R.C.Gorman

The Lithographs

DESERT WOMEN July 1976 Multi-color 22 x 30 inches Editions Press

R.C.Gorman

The Lithographs

BY DORIS MONTHAN
with a Foreword by Jules Heller

 NORTHLAND PRESS / FLAGSTAFF

To my sister
Trudi Born McShane

Contents

Foreword

GIVEN A MAKER OF IMAGES, a rock formed eons ago in the dark depths of the earth, a greasy crayon or a liquid substance containing grease held in suspension, and a meaningful visual idea; given an individual who wishes to share with numbers of people that fleeting, wispy, ephemeral, slippery idea skipping around in his or her head; given someone like R. C. Gorman who relishes the sensuousness of working on a limestone surface, who enjoys, revels in, and feels compelled to draw that which he knows, has experienced, feels deeply; given all of these conditions — a lithograph may be birthed.

Between that birth and the finished edition of a particular lithograph lie myriad and wondrous phenomena, people, and extraordinary skills and talents. Of all the graphic arts mediums, lithography (I admit my bias freely, and without reservation) is the most challenging, the most satisfying, the most rewarding, the most responsive for artists. The lithographic stone returns multiple originals from that which is drawn, brushed, scratched, or engraved upon its surface, after it is chemically treated and appropriately printed. The stone may be likened unto a permanent sheet of paper on which one may work in any style, using any grease-laden material, to express visually that which demands expression.

About 180 years B.T. (Before Tamarind), *stone printing* was invented by Alois Senefelder (1771–1834), a Bavarian actor, author, student of law; a man desirous of using his many talents and interests (including more than a basic knowledge of chemistry) to earn a decent living. Through much trial and more error, in the course of searching to find cheaper ways of printing his plays and other materials, Senefelder perfected chemical printing from stone. For reasons not germane to this brief essay, we call Senefelder's invention *lithography*. It marked a giant step forward in the world of commercial printing, and artists soon became aware of its potential as a medium. Within twenty years of the technique's "invention," lithographic workshops were founded in England, France, Austria, Germany, Italy, Spain, Russia, and the United States — and some of these workshops encouraged collaboration with artists of the stature of Benjamin West and Francisco Goya, to name but two of the earliest "superstars."

Except for the advent of offset lithography (wherein the drawn image on a lithographic plate, grained to imitate a stone, is first printed on to a rubber blanket and then set off on the sheet of paper) Senefelder, by and large, described the entire process, as still practiced today, in his own text written in 1817. What *is* the process of lithography? What *is* this deep, dark "secret" guarded so carefully, by so many, for so long that, as short a time ago as 1950 when working on my book *Printmaking Today*, few, if any, "professional" printers would care to disclose information of any sort about their several approaches to the medium; none wished to share that which he believed he *alone* knew — that grease and water do not mix; since you drew with grease, treated the stone chemically, and kept it wet with water, the greasy ink was only accepted by the grease-drawn areas and was repelled by the undrawn parts of the stone. Fortunately, adolescent thinking sometimes matures and information about lithography is readily available to all — *as it always was* since the nineteenth century, to those who but cared to read. Briefly, assuming one has access to the tools, materials, and presses requisite for making lithographs, or if one has sufficient monies with which to purchase time and professional labor in a professional printmaking workshop, the procedure is elementary.

There is this "something" you want desperately to draw on stone, so special that it must be multiplied by the lithographic process into an edition of a certain number. You have made the necessary arrangements. You or someone else grind the surface of a beautiful blue gray limestone, about four inches thick, with various grades of carborundum and water until the surface of that stone begs to be caressed by the lithographic crayons and tusche at your side. You begin to draw. . . . It is finished.

After dusting powdered resin and French chalk on the drawing, an "etch" of nitric acid and gum arabic is brushed all over the stone. It does not truly etch anything, but that is what we call it. It does create a slight effervescence on the stone, after some moments. This etch that is not an etch is wiped down on the stone to a fine, even film and fanned dry. At this juncture, the drawn parts of the image have been made more receptive to ink and the undrawn parts protected from the ink to be used in printing. The gum plays other roles as well.

Using lithotine (a solvent), the gummed stone is then flooded and washed until the drawing "disappears" from the surface. Water follows and the surface of the stone will remain continually wet until printing begins. (If one looks very carefully, at a particular angle to the stone, it is possible to make out the "ghost" of what one drew, lying there, in wait to be protected by a layer of ink — in the same manner and to the same degree that it was drawn.) Thus, delicate grays will accept only tiny amounts of ink; rich, solid, velvety blacks will accept amounts of ink equal to the quantity of grease drawn thereon.

The lithographic roller is charged with a specially prepared ink and passed over the ink slab again and again. You can hear the peculiar hissing sound made by the correct amount of ink and lithographic varnish as the roller travels back and forth over the slab. Now, the roller is passed over the drawing on the stone, which has just been wiped carefully with two water-wet sponges. Slowly the drawing begins to appear on the surface of the stone as though from behind a filmy cloud. It becomes clearer and clearer until it is ready to be proofed. Each proof allows certain manipulation which comes closer to the artist's goal. At a certain stage, you say, "Now!" And this proof becomes the *bon a tirer*, the standard by which all prints in the edition will be measured. Thus are lithographs made. Thus have they been made — with variations supplied by each maker! Thus will they be made in the future.

The world of lithography is an unofficial fraternity. Although we have never met, I share with R. C. Gorman the experience of Mexico's murals, artists, and printers including Raul Anguiano, José Sanchez, and so many others who once made lithographs and relief prints at the Taller de Gráfica Popular in Mexico City. Gorman's lithographs of Navajo women, in my view, rank among his best works. Here, the principle that "less is more" is meaningful. His line is a visual delight to track; it expresses love on a stone.

JULES HELLER
Dean, College of Fine Arts
Arizona State University

Preface

BEFORE THIS BOOK was formally announced, when it was just casually mentioned to people in the art field, the uniform reaction was: "It's long overdue!" Despite the fact that only a handful of books devoted to an individual Indian artist have been published, it seemed natural that R. C. Gorman would be among the first candidates for a book of his own.

As long ago as 1968, when Gorman was just on the brink of nationwide recognition, an article in the *Indian Historian* notes: "Strongly a Navajo man, R. C. Gorman is above all an artist. He is also a raconteur, traveler, music lover, literature enthusiast — cosmopolitan to the core — and Indian in the most all-embracing sense. Such a combination of qualities and proclivities has produced a unique and fascinating personality. One day someone will surely write 'The Story of R. C. Gorman.' It is inevitable."[1]

In the ten years since that was published, Gorman has been the subject of countless newspaper and magazine articles and has been included in a number of books. I first met him in 1971 when my husband, Guy, and I were just beginning to select artists for our book, *Art and Indian Individualists.* We had seen some of Gorman's work, and when discussing possible artists with museum people and private collectors, Gorman was always among the first artists suggested. In the summer of 1971 we stopped at his Navajo Gallery in Taos. The gallery had an appealing ambiance about it — sunlight flooding in the large windows set in thick adobe walls; paintings everywhere, yet not intruding; one of his many cats rubbing against our legs; a constant flow of people, mostly friends and other artists, the informal atmosphere of a home. One had the desire to sit down and visit for a while, which is just what we did. Gorman was friendly and casual; there were many laughs, as we discovered there always would be when in his company. He was spectacular looking, with patrician features centered in a broad expanse of face with wide, high cheekbones. He wore dramatic clothes and a brightly colored headband. As Dr.

Harry Wood noted in an article some three years later: "He wears his headband like a 40-karat gold crown."[2] Gorman's personality and manner of dressing are always fascinating topics to those who write about him. In the same year we met him, Robert A. Ewing had written in *New Mexico Magazine:* "Gorman is controversial and contradictory. He can be a colorful showman draped in turquoise and silver or the gentle and helpful friend in need to a young Indian artist."[3]

On subsequent visits my husband photographed several of his Navajo blanket paintings. Among the works displayed in his gallery then was his 1970 lithograph *Three Taos Men,* but at that time there was more interest in his paintings. Gorman had suggested we contact Dr. Byron C. Butler of Phoenix, as he had many of his works. We did that fall and photographed a number of paintings from his extensive collection. The following March we attended the first showing of Gorman's Tamarind lithographs which Dr. Butler had published. It was then we became aware of lithography as a viable medium for him. This it certainly has proven to be. Since then he has produced over a hundred editions, a total of between five and six thousand lithographs. So popular have his lithographs become that they now comprise a major portion of his artistic production, and it is likely that more people have come to know him through his lithographs than any of the other mediums in which he works.

So many people have contributed to the producing of this book that I can only thank them in general in the space allotted here. Information for the text came from many sources. For providing valuable new material, I am deeply indebted to Marilyn Butler. Between August 20 and 24 of 1973, she taped a series of interviews with Gorman's mother, John Manchester and other friends. Though the book project she had planned was abandoned soon after, she retained the tapes, and graciously turned them over to me for use in this book. Most were in good condition, and after transcribing them, I found a great deal that would add to the text. Of particular value were those made from conversations with Gorman's mother, who died in late 1973. Gorman's father, Carl Nelson Gorman, gave me excellent material which I could not have obtained from other sources and, in addition, made helpful suggestions and corrections on the finished manuscript. Another fine source was Grace Davis McCullah, Gorman's cousin. Dr. Byron Butler, who played such a vital role in Gorman's lithographic career, was helpful in countless ways and loaned a number of lithographs from his collection for reproduction in the book. The lithographers with whom Gorman has collaborated in recent years were very accommodating and provided both technical information and personal anecdotes, much of which is quoted in the text. From Tamarind Institute I received detailed information on Gorman's five-year period of production there from Judith Booth, assistant director, and some helpful suggestions from Clinton Adams, director of the institute and co-author of *The Tamarind Book of Lithography: Art and Techniques*. Finally, I am especially grateful to Jules Heller, dean of the College of Fine Arts, Arizona State University and the earliest exponent of the university-based lithographic workshop on the West Coast, for contributing a foreword which communicates all the excitement inherent in the producing of a fine lithograph.

Author's Note: The lithographs are grouped under the year in which printing was completed. Some are not arranged chronologically within the year for technical reasons. In the case of suites of lithographs, the completion of printing for the last lithograph in the suite determines the year under which the suite appears.

x

THE ARTIST

A Biography of
R.C. Gorman

THE EARLY YEARS 1932–1942

IF AN ARTIST could choose his birthplace, he could find no more dramatic or compelling spot than historic Canyon de Chelly. Located on the Navajo Reservation in the northeastern part of Arizona, it is an awe-inspiring memorial to one of the oldest civilizations in the country, containing over two thousand prehistoric sites and twelve major ruins. The quality of its light, so vital to an artist's inspiration, is unrivaled by any other place in the world. When touched by the rising and setting sun, its thousand-foot-high sandstone cliffs blaze with rich magentas, warm peach tones, pinks, yellows, and deep golds. Of it can truly be said: "You make the places where morning and evening have birth to shout for joy."[4]

Cradled in its steep cliffs are the three-story-high, ninety-room apartment dwellings which housed the Anasazi, "the ancient ones," for almost ten centuries. In these dwellings the Anasazi left remnants of their rich and remarkable civilization — beautiful garments of spun cotton, shell and feathers; copper bells and flutes; beads and turquoise; baskets and sandals. On the walls of the canyon they left pictures, painted and pecked, of animals, humans, and mythic symbols. To this day rumors persist that the spirits of "the ancient ones" still hover there — one can hear their whispers, the rustle of their garments everywhere, it is said.

It was in Canyon de Chelly among the spirits of "the ancient ones" that the Navajo lived and continue to live today. In the winter of 1864, however, they were driven from their beautiful canyon by United States military forces — saw their homes, sheep and horses and prize peach orchards destroyed. The Navajos were taken on The Long Walk, some three hundred miles to Fort Sumner at the Bosque Redondo in New Mexico. After four years of imprisonment and hundreds of deaths from cold, hunger, and disease, the great Navajo chief, Manuelito, and twelve other chiefs signed a peace treaty, and in 1868, the Navajos were allowed to return to their homeland, now cut to about one-fourth of its original size. For them it was the beginning of reservation life.[5]

One of those who survived The Long Walk, the internment at Fort Sumner, and the return journey was Peshlakai, the paternal great-grandfather of R. C. Gorman. Sixty-four years later, on July 26, 1932, his great-grandson was born at Chinle, Arizona, just at the mouth of Canyon de Chelly, at the point where its many branches begin fanning out toward the east.

Rudolph Carl Gorman was the son of Carl Nelson Gorman and Adella Katherine Brown. The name "Rudolph" was soon abandoned, and though he is still known as 'Rudy" by family and childhood friends, he began signing his art "R. C." more than twenty-five years ago, and that is the name by which he is best known today.

Life on the Navajo Reservation had never been affluent, but during those grim Depression years while Gorman was growing up it was stark, and he often knew hunger. One did not see a pickup truck parked at every hogan as one does today. The automobile was a rarity, and to an impressionable child, a thing of beauty and glamour. It, along with Mickey Mouse, were Gorman's favorite subjects when he first began drawing at the age of three. At this time there was little contact with the world beyond the reservation, and these may have been the only "Anglo" cultural expressions which had filtered through. At any rate, they held great fascination for him. He and his cousin, Billy, who was later to become a medicine man, drew them endlessly, using as their materials a stick and the dirt floor of the hogan. Since there was no electricity, they often drew by the light of a kerosene lamp, and on nice days they would draw outside in the red sands of Canyon de Chelly.

Several years ago when Gorman was asked what his first materials had been, he answered: "Sand, rocks, mud," and added, "You know Chinle Wash? Well, when the water comes out of the canyon at Chinle, when there is lots of it, when it's flooding — then, as it recedes it leaves the most beautiful muddy places. That's the best place to draw pictures on, put your bare feet in it and see the patterns they leave. Sometimes I used my hands to draw in it or a stick. That's where I did my first sculptures, too, fashioning them out of mud — Mickey mouse, cars, and later airplanes. I went through an airplane period."

In those early years he never had crayons, coloring books, or any of the slick, commercial toys that are enjoyed by children today, or for that matter, the toys many children had during the 1930s, but this, to him, was not a hardship. "The Navajo child has to make his own toys, at least he did when I was growing up, so the creative approach becomes natural to him and allows him to express himself in many mediums."

There was work to be done, too. As with most Navajo children he was sent out early to herd the family sheep. His cousin, Grace Davis McCullah, notes: "We all lived pretty much the same; one hogan was not so different from another. The only way you could tell a family's wealth was by their livestock, how much they had. If they had cattle and horses in addition to sheep, they were considered well-off."

Where Gorman was rich was in his ancestry and the culture imparted through it. His talents, one feels, had evolved through generations of exceptional people. Among his ancestors on both sides of the family were sandpainters, silversmiths, and weavers. There were chanters, a long line of holy men, and the famous Navajo chief, Manuelito. His paternal grandparents founded the first Presbyterian Mission at Chinle. His grandmother translated thirty-one hymns into Navajo that are still in use today. She was also an expert weaver who taught other Navajo women in the craft. Of the paternal great-grandfather, Peshlakai, who had survived The Long Walk, Carl N. Gorman says: "He was a great leader. At Fort Sumner he learned how to work in silver and when he returned he taught many other Navajos silvermaking — so many that he almost had an assembly line going. The family use the spelling 'Peshlakai' as a surname, but his full Navajo name was *Beshthlagai ilthini althtsosigi*, meaning Slender Maker of Silver."

Peshlakai was known as an "innovator of new forms."[6] Both Chee Dodge, another Navajo leader, and the Franciscan fathers considered him to be "one of the best, if not the best silversmith in the tribe."[7] In 1893 he accompanied Lieutenant Edward H. Plummer to the Chicago World's Fair and returned with liberal attitudes toward education, which he championed. He also acted as a mediator between the United States government and his people. In 1970 the *Navajo Times* featured an article on him, noting: "Because of his many talents, Peshlakai was one of the great men in Navajo history. In the opinion of Father Berard Haile of Saint Michael's, the silversmith's influence dominated the Navajo more than any other man at the time, and at his

death on December 10, 1915, there was deep grief felt among all the Navajos."[8]

Another facet of Gorman's ancestral heritage was his clan affiliation. As Grace McCullah noted in explaining her relationship to R. C.: "We are related both by blood and by clan, but among the Navajo the clan relationship is the most important." Carl Gorman's clan was *Debé lizhíni*, meaning Black Sheep. This was his mother's clan, for as he points out, "We belong to our mother's clan. My father's clan was *Khinya áni*, the Towering House People, so I am son to all the *Khinya áni*. It was the first named of the four original clans." According to the Navajo creation myth it was they who came up first from the underworld.

Gorman's mother's clan, and thus, his clan, is the *Tl'ashchí*. There is some dispute over its English translation. The Franciscan fathers in their *Ethnologic Dictionary of the Navajo Language* interpret it as "Red Lefties," so named because the soil of their country was bright red and they were left-handed.[9] Gorman says that the story told him by his Aunt Mary was: "A war had been fought and a baby had been left behind. A Navajo woman recovered the child and noticed that it had a red bottom. This could have been a migratory settler's child that had been abandoned, but, anyway, the child was adopted by the Navajo and they started a new clan for it — the 'Red Bottom' clan." Gorman's mother denied this, saying *Tl'ashchí* simply meant "captured" or "adopted." Whatever the true translation, Gorman delighted in teasing her about it. His mother noted: "The *Tl'ashchí* are people that are very progressive. They don't have a hard time in living like some others. That's the way they're considered, that good luck always comes their way." Her father's clan was the *Hashtl'íshni*, the Mud People, a branch of one of the four main clans. His mother said: "They're very comical people, so outspoken and not bashful — that's the way they're considered. They're always saying something funny."

It is likely that Gorman's wit and sense of humor came from the characteristics of this grandfather and his clan. No doubt his personality traits and wide-ranging intelligence came from both sides of the family, but it was from his father that one suspects he inherited his artistic talent. Born in 1907, Carl Nelson Gorman was one of the first Indian artists to depart from the traditional style of painting and to lead other artists toward a more personal expression. He is one of the few well-known Indian artists of his generation who was not trained at the Santa Fe Indian School and one of the first to receive college-level training at a strictly Anglo-oriented art institution. Following service with the marines in the South Pacific during World War II as a member of the famous "Navajo Code Talkers," he attended Otis Art Institute in Los Angeles and had further study under such distinguished artists as Norman Rockwell, Nicolai Fechin, and Joseph Magnaini. He worked as a commercial artist in Southern California and later held a number of positions on the reservation. For four years, beginning

4

in 1970, he lectured on Navajo history and culture, as well as art, at the University of California at Davis, where a museum on campus has been named for him. He has done considerable research on all aspects of Navajo culture and has written and lectured extensively on the subject. Currently he is coordinator of Navajo Resources, Curriculum Development for Navajo Studies at the Navajo Community College at Tsaile, Arizona.

In his painting he has worked in a variety of styles, none of them resembling R. C.'s. In fact, people seeing his work often do not connect him with his famous son, since Carl Gorman has always signed his work *Kin-ya-onny beyeh*, meaning "Son to the Towering House People." (He uses the Anglicized spelling.) However, when he began doing lithographs in 1977 he signed them "Carl N. Gorman" and plans to use this signature in the future.

R. C., however, has sometimes said, "My father did not really influence my art, mainly because he was gone during most of my growing-up years during the war." Recently, he recalled: "My daddy had some job out on the reservation, away from home, and I went to stay with him for a time. I was maybe seven or eight at the time. We usually ate our meals outdoors on the ground. My daddy would cook fried potatoes and I remember how he would spread wax paper or just a brown paper grocery bag on the ground and place the cold canned beans and other food on it. I always remember how he served it so ceremoniously. That's the only time I remember being with my daddy alone during my early childhood before he went away to the war."

His cousin Grace notes: "His parents separated when he was quite young. It was always Aunt Adella [R. C.'s mother] that I remember during our childhood."

And this leads to the women who had perhaps the greatest influence on his early years and who remain his favorite subject matter. If he has a "signature work" it is his Navajo women, placidly going about their business of building fires, picking corn, nursing babies, walking across the desert, or, more often, majestically reclining with an enviable serenity. They transmit to the viewer a dignity and timelessness that proclaims: "We are, we always have been, we always will be." It is this strength and sense of security which the women in his early life gave to Gorman. They were strong women, as evidenced by his great-grandmother who undertook his care at birth. As Gorman tells it: "My mother had been in labor for twenty-four hours at the Chinle hospital, and I was born prematurely. I was so frail and sickly at birth that I was placed in an incubator, but even there I guess I was barely surviving. I was told that when my great-grandmother came to see me, she took one look and said to my mother: 'These crazy white people are killing your child!' My mother tells me my great-grandmother threatened the doctors and nurses, waving her juniper cane at them, and demanded my release from the hospital." Apparently, she prevailed, for they allowed her to take him home, where she put him on a good sensi-ble Navajo diet of goat's milk and coffee. Under her care he thrived. "I was told that soon I became quite heavy." Forty-three years later he paid tribute to her in the KAET/ Phoenix film on him: "The women in my life are my charcoal. They are soft and strong like my great-grandmother who gave me life."[10]

It was his maternal grandmother, however, who was the greatest influence. His mother recalls: "Rudy always wanted to go herding sheep with his grandmother. When he was about ten years old, I used to take him to my mother's sheep camp. That was at Waterless Mountain between Black Mesa and Hopi country. We had a lot of rocks there, and when he was out herding sheep, his grandmother told me he would draw on a rock with another rock. I guess those rocks were just like a blackboard to him. His cousins tell me those drawings he did on the rocks are still there."

It was this grandmother who raised him. Gorman says of her: "My grandmother introduced me to beauty." She undertook R. C.'s education in Navajo lore, told him the Navajo legends and sang the old songs to him which had been passed down from generation to generation. When they herded sheep, she would point out the various plants — which were good to eat, which were bad, and those which had medicinal powers. On warm summer evenings, lying on the ground, she pointed out the stars, giving him the Navajo name for each, how they came to be fixed in their positions in the sky according to Navajo myths, and how a Navajo should always point at a rainbow with his thumb. This was delicious fare for the imagination of a young child, and Gorman credits her with his early ambition to become a writer.

His mother, on the other hand, directed him toward the Anglo world and spoke to him only in English. She was oriented toward the present, but in the 1973 interview when discussing Navajo clan names and their origins, she expressed her regret in not having learned more about her Navajo heritage: "Oh, I wish I had talked to my mother more about these things, or to my grandmother. I didn't know it was going to be so important in the future — now when my children and their friends ask me about them." She further explained: "I guess then I wasn't interested in the past, because when I was sent to the state school at the age of five I didn't know a word of English. I had a hard time till they sent me away to Sherman Institute where they had all kinds of tribes. I didn't have a chance to talk Navajo, so that's how I had to learn English — from other tribes. Many already could speak English — like the Mission Indians only did speak English because they had mixed with white people and Spanish people all their lives. Indians here didn't have a chance to live with white people. That's what made me make up my mind — I wasn't going to have my kids have a hard time with learning their English. I wanted them to be able to get along in the world, so when I had my kids, I spoke to them in English first. If they heard Navajo, they heard it from someone else."

This early training in the English language could account for the fact that Gorman is a prodigious reader, as well as a talented writer. It also prepared him for his first schooling. His mother recalled: "I sent him to Chinle Public School when he was about five-and-a-half years old. Right away they put him in first grade because he already knew his ABC's and numbers." She added: "I remember that first day I sent him to school he was just crying. He said he was scared to go to school. The next day I asked the teacher how he got along and she said he slept all afternoon. He was used to taking a nap in the afternoon at home. I had to laugh." The afternoon nap is a habit Gorman has never outgrown and may come as a surprise to those who marvel at his energy the rest of the day and night.

He attended Chinle Public School through the fourth grade, and most of his memories of it are pleasant. In speaking of his first store-bought art materials, he says: "My earliest recollection is a plain, old pencil and lined writing tablet. Then when I went to school they supplied us with . . . crayons . . . clay . . . colored paper." He draws out the words, lingers over them, and a child-like quality creeps into his voice, recapturing the wonder and delight he must really have felt in using these marvelous new tools.

As to his early art efforts in school, his mother remembered: "When he was still quite small, he would bring art home from school, drawings of pretty ladies, just like cartoons. That's the only thing I used to notice. Of course, I didn't know anything about art at that time." However, she did administer criticism of his art on one occasion — when he did a drawing of a naked woman. For this, he received a whipping at school and, when his mother found out about it, from her also.

Whether anyone else was impressed with his early art efforts or not, Gorman took himself seriously as an artist from the very beginning. His father recalls: "When Rudy was six years old, he came to visit me one day while I was working for the government's Navajo stock and sheep program. We were dipping sheep way out at Navajo Mountain, near Kaibito. Rudy came out where we were working. He brought his pad and pencil with him and asked one of the Navajo girls there to pose for him and proceeded to draw a picture of her. The workers who watched were amused by that and often talked about it later."

Apparently, the whipping received for one of his first art efforts did not stifle Gorman's creative inclination, for his father recalls that five or six years later, "Rudy was staying at his grandmother's sheep camp and one day drew a large nude lady on one of the rocks there. His aunt gave him a good scolding for it. She never realized that someday his drawings of ladies would make him famous!"

NEW INFLUENCES 1942–1950

DURING WORLD WAR II, many Navajos were sent to

Flagstaff, Arizona, to work in the Navajo Ordinance. Gorman, who was ten at the time, remembers that he and his mother were shipped there in cattle cars. "We were tough people then. Indians today would be indignant at such treatment."

But he also remembers that "on the way to Flagstaff we stopped in Hopiland at Moencopi Trading Post and I saw my first painting. It was by a Hopi artist. There were several landscape paintings and I thought they were the most beautiful things I had ever seen. After that they were always vivid in my mind and I wished I could do that, too." In Flagstaff, he attended public school, where, he says, "We were told what to draw, which didn't do much for me."

When he was twelve, his mother sent him to Saint Michael's, a Catholic boarding school. It was part of the Franciscan Mission on the Navajo Reservation at the eastern border of Arizona. "He didn't like it," she said. Gorman puts it less mildly: "That was the only time in my life that I remember being constantly hungry. The nuns gave only the big boys milk with their meals. We smaller ones made bean sandwiches at the table and sneaked them out to eat later. I remember that a sheep there had a lamb that was born dead, and a friend of mine and I butchered it secretly. A nun took pity on us and cooked it for us, and we hid away and ate the whole thing. I also picked up lice at Saint Michael's. I was baptized a Catholic when I went there, and I remember walking to mass before dawn every morning with icicles forming in my hair. I had quite a few unpleasant encounters with those holy ladies. Looking back on it now, I can see that the fault wasn't all on the part of the school; it just wasn't the place for me." His mother had said she didn't send him back there the next year, to which Gorman added, "I was expelled."

"After Saint Michael's" his mother notes, "I thought I would try sending him to Ganado, the Presbyterian Mission school. It was the best school on the reservation. I had to pay to send him there. I didn't have much money to spend, but still I sent him. It was a boarding school, too. He was very sad when I left him. I guess he didn't want me to leave him there by himself, but there were a lot of other boys like him, and one of them came along and took him inside. I didn't know how he got along there; he never told me at the time, but later he said it was the best school he ever attended."

The Ganado Presbyterian Mission School was remarkable in its day and outstanding by today's standards. The Presbyterian Church had begun its mission work at Ganado in 1901 and had several classes in progress that same year. The noted Indian trader, Don Lorenzo Hubbell, had a trading post there (now an historic site), and though a Roman Catholic, helped the Presbyterian Church secure title to 100 acres for the mission and later helped secure another 100 acres for mission use. He also provided housing and transportation for the missionaries until they had their own.[11] When Dr. Clarence G. Salsbury arrived there in 1927, he found a stone church, five or six adobe buildings, and several small residences. Dr. Salsbury, who had served as a medical missionary in China for twelve years, found many similarities between the Chinese and the Navajos,[12] and soon established a rapport with his new patients and students, who came to know him affectionately as "Dr. Tso" (Dr. Big). He served as director of education, director of the hospital and nursing school, as well as physician, counselor, and advisor to the students and the entire Navajo population in an area that covered 26,000 square miles. By the time Gorman arrived in 1945, Ganado Mission was a self-sufficient modern community with some fifty buildings, a central powerhouse, and a farming complex where almost all of the mission's food was raised.[13]

Dr. Salsbury had had a series of colorful jobs while putting himself through the College of Physicians and Surgeons in Boston — as an artist's model, photographer, and a "super" in theatrical productions. Years later, he said: "Show business never left my blood: Our Christmas parties at the mission were always filled with skits and pageantry."[14] He encouraged all the arts at Ganado School.

This provided an ideal environment for Gorman's talents to flourish. He was fortunate on another level, too: In the 1940s it was said that only one Navajo child in four would be able to go to school. As one of his teachers, Barbara Anderson, notes: "Those who were in school were there because they had background, ability, and determination. The majority of Rudy's classmates in the class of 1950 are truly successful human beings. None has become as well known as Rudy, but they have held responsible positions both on and off the reservation."

Elma Smith, another teacher, affirms this: "All of our graduates made something of themselves." She is a good example for she, herself, was one of the school's graduates and went on to become the first Navajo to graduate from the University of Arizona (in 1941), and later received her master's degree. She notes: "Each student had two or three hours of work assigned to him each day: some worked in the laundry, others swept the dormitories, any work which needed to be done."

Gorman remembers: "My favorite job was working at the barn. I milked the cows and loved it! I worked with Kenny Douthitt, the minister's son. Getting up at 4:30 every morning gives one a certain discipline — especially when it's freezing cold."

Elma further noted, "Rudy was an artist even way back then and was always jolly and outgoing."

Gorman's cousin, Grace Davis McCullah, who is another one of the school's outstanding graduates, received her B.A. in political science from Arizona State University and is now executive director of the Indian Development District of Arizona. She notes: "Rudy and I went through Ganado High School together. He was a brilliant kid — his sense of humor, his imagination. I remember he liked to fool around with music and was always composing. I played

the piano, so he wanted me to play the tunes he made up and write the music down. It was so frustrating to him that I wasn't able to do all this."

Though his musical ambitions were thwarted, Gorman was finding expression in other fields. Barbara Anderson recalls: "Rudy had arrived at Ganado the year before I did. Teacher Elizabeth Young, who arrived the same year he did, said that all the teachers kind of stood in awe of this little kid in the eighth grade who could draw anything on the blackboard, and who had the vocabulary to discuss it."

Gorman remembers that every Christmas he was asked to draw the Nativity scene on the blackboard. This may have originated one of his favorite and most enduring themes — the "Madonna," or "mother and child."

Barbara Anderson has many "Rudy vignettes" which "brightened a teacher's day." At the same time they reveal much about Gorman, the teenager: "When I was teaching, my husband said to me one day, 'You talk about Rudy all the time.' My answer was, 'If you had Rudy in three classes every day, you would talk about him, too.' That year I had him in English 3 and in Spanish 2. And he came to the Spanish 1 class every day for review — his own idea.

"There is no doubt but that he was different. He read everything from opera to classics to popular fiction. One day in class he sat engrossed in Old Jules by Mari Sandoz. Suddenly he blurted out, 'This guy married six ladies!' Every boy in the class read the book in the next few weeks.

"To illustrate a point in a grammar lesson, he wrote the following sentence: 'By four o'clock I shall have murdered Miss Verna Keams [a student Gorman was feuding with at the time].'

"For a letter-writing assignment, he wrote to his father asking for money. He signed it, 'Your insistent son.'

"In the fall of 1948, the school held a mock election. Rudy was Henry Wallace, the Progressive candidate. He did not win. The school paper reported, 'The Republican Party had the most in numbers, but the Progressive Party made the most noise.' The whole school was crestfallen the next day to hear that Truman had won. Dr. Salsbury was a staunch Republican, as were the Hubbells, and it was a great revelation to the student body that these pillars of their isolated community did not have all the answers. Rudy was particularly vocal in his disappointment that Dr. Salsbury would not be Indian Commissioner after all.

"Rudy was never a discipline problem, but rather, he was easy to work with, well adjusted, well liked, and definitely a leader. He was interested in everything. He composed songs, wrote plays. He wrote, produced, directed, and acted in his senior play.

"I believe we must have given him excellence, vision, and a certain kind of freedom despite the rather rigid rules of a boarding school in those days. He was fortunate in having remarkable fellow students. Looking back, I think this was the key to his blossoming at Ganado. Those young people provided a fertile, receptive atmosphere in which a creative talent like Rudy's could thrive."

And thrive it did! In addition to his many exploratory ventures into other areas of creativity during his high school years, it was there that his true vocation was solidified. The impetus came from a remarkable little woman: "My art instructor at Ganado was Jenny Louis Lind. She had volunteered to teach art to us — that's the kind of person she was. She encouraged me to do what I felt like doing. That was the first time I ever painted in oils."

Up to this point, most of Gorman's knowledge of painting had come from books. "I read the book about Beatien Yazz, *Spin a Silver Dollar*, and that impressed me. I saw some of his illustrations and I thought they were great. I sort of wanted to be like him at that time. I even tried to paint in his style. I still have a painting I did around then — two little fat, chubby boys in a tree. Then there were some of the other Indian artists, the traditionalists, and I tried painting like them, but Jenny Louis Lind never insisted I paint that way or any other way. She encouraged me to try everything."

He has very few unhappy memories from these years, but there is one incident he has never forgotten: "When I was in ninth or tenth grade, I took some of my paintings to a woman at a trading post in Gallup and she sold them. When I went back to get my money, she said 'What money?' I've often wondered how many other people she treated that way." The incident helped to shape some of his attitudes concerning the business side of art. He can be shrewd about selling and promoting his own art; yet, always ready to help and guide young artists in selling theirs.

Recently, Gorman observed: "In high school you are easily influenced, and I was lucky in having the kind of teachers I did." When he graduated from Ganado High School in 1950, he was near the top of his class. Teacher Barbara Anderson, writing in 1978, said: "I don't know 'R. C.,' but I did know 'Rudy' very well, and I expect he is still very much there behind the 'R. C.'" As with most adults, this is true; unlike most, however, Gorman has kept in touch — with Dr. Salsbury and many of his teachers. Some twenty years after graduating, he continued to pay visits to his art teacher, Jenny Louis Lind, whenever he was near her home, and he still says, "She was probably the greatest influence on my life."

TRAVEL AND TRAINING 1950–1963

AFTER GRADUATING from Ganado High School, Gorman went to Flagstaff where his mother was still living. He decided to go on to college and enrolled at Arizona State College (now Northern Arizona University). At that point, Gorman said, "I wanted to do a lot of things. I took it for granted that I was an artist, but it didn't occur to me that I might make a living with my art. So I thought I'd be a dentist or a merchant seaman or an airline pilot. The reason that none of those worked out was because I was so bad at

math. The only figures I understand are nude figures."

The Korean War was then in progress, and in 1951, he enlisted in the navy. "That," he says, "was my first introduction to the outside world." It was the first time he had been off the reservation for any long period and the first time he had ever traveled beyond the borders of Arizona and New Mexico. "I loved the navy. I was in it four years. It was a tremendous education — so many men from so many backgrounds; yet, I had a real sense of belonging."

He was first stationed in San Diego and then shipped out to the Mariana Islands where he served with the Fleet Aircraft Service Squadron. One of the men he met there was Ronn Rutt, now a professional photographer in Bethlehem, Pennsylvania. Gorman notes: "We still communicate and visit each other."

While in the Marianas they both attended classes at Guam Territorial College, a branch of Ohio State. Rutt recalls: "We took journalism and English because at that time we both wanted to be writers, but R. C. never stopped drawing. I often modeled for him — he would sketch my hands, nose, feet, whatever he was trying to master at the time. Now I often attend his shows and photograph him and his art for various publications."

Gorman's art talents in the service, however, were directed mostly toward what might be called "commercial art." He earned "quite a lot of money" by painting or drawing pictures of the men's wives or girl friends. "They would give me photographs, usually just a head-and-shoulders shot; I would copy that and then draw a Petty Girl or Varga-style figure under it. The men loved it. I usually charged the officers seven dollars and the enlisted men, two."

After his discharge in 1955, he returned to Flagstaff and enrolled at Northern Arizona University for the second time. "I just couldn't go back to the reservation to live again. I appreciate the beautiful country and loved my mother but I'm not a sentimentalist and I knew I couldn't return to it." At the university he majored in literature and took art as a minor. He still had dreams of becoming a writer and "I was seriously thinking of becoming a teacher." He took several art courses from Ellery Gibson and the late John Salter, both of whom he still admires.

He illustrated a magazine article Gibson wrote for *School Arts Magazine*, which was published in the June, 1956, issue. The article's humorous slant was well-matched by Gorman's four cartoons, illustrating children's ways of seeing things, often very different from what the teacher expects. Gorman is still proud of this first national publication of his art, and it was a happy collaboration as far as Gibson was concerned. Recently, he said, "Rudy was a delightful kid to have in class. There was never a dull moment with him around."

Gorman did not complete his studies for a teacher's degree. "As I began to sell a lot of my work, I changed my mind." He had become more sophisticated in his attitudes toward art. As he said, "Where I was raised we didn't have museums, anything like that. The only influence I had during my early years came from books." He had gone through his "traditional Indian style" in high school. Since that time he had seen considerably more, both in books and in museums. "My first great interest was Rembrandt. Another time I was terribly moved by Salvador Dali — by his technique. Also, before Dali, was van Gogh. I even went through a Gauguin period. I think the influence from these artists were mostly technique and then, of course, color. Dali knows just what to do with color. And Rembrandt creates mood, and van Gogh, there again it's color, but also the wild excitement of rhythm — color chasing color, flying, colliding, exploding. Those are all influences I felt."

But the great impact was to come. "I had been taken to Mexico on a trip and I was really turned on. It's the only place where museums had impressed me — where the painting overwhelmed me. The first time I saw Orozco, I could hardly believe it. It was close to me, close to my people. I confess I have been bored by the paintings of the great classic painters that you see in most museums. But there — Orozco, Rivera, Siqueiros — these were real people painting real people!"

Upon his return, Gorman went to his father's home in Encino, California, and from there applied for a grant from the Navajo Tribal Council for study in Mexico. In 1958 he was awarded a scholarship, the only one the council has given for study outside the United States. He studied at Mexico City College (now the University of the Americas). But it was exposure to the works of the great Mexican masters — Orozco, Rivera, Siqueiros, Tamayo, Anguiano — that made R. C. abandon his "Indian way of painting.

"I would have to have been stupid not to be influenced by those Mexican painters," he says. "When they made an impression, they made a huge impression. Orozco's mural in the Cabañas Institute at Guadalajara — there's a greatness there that takes your breath away."

Many years later, he observed: "Rivera was like a wordy historian — he was painting for people who couldn't read or write. With Siqueiros and Orozco you had to know a little more Mexican history to know what they are saying. Orozco, with just a few strokes of his brush, makes a whole lot of explosive revelations."[15] In some ways it seems strange that the apolitical Gorman should be so attracted to Orozco, Rivera, and Siqueiros. But when one considers that they were not only rebelling against a corrupt government, but against, what they considered, the decadent art prevailing in Mexico during the nineteenth and early twentieth century, it makes more sense. Gormon, too, was rebelling — against traditional Indian painting; neither could he identify with the European masters nor those in the mainstream of American art. When he went to Mexico, he was struggling to find his own expression; the Mexican painters opened the door. Perhaps, it was that these artists had rediscovered their own Indianness — that Gorman

may have felt a link with them deep in the caverns of the past, primordial images and archetypes in the collective Indian unconscious. At any rate, it was a case of instant recognition, and their works served as a catalyst for releasing his own artistic inclination and Indian heritage. In a 1972 interview with Gerald Theisen he said: "Rivera went to Europe to discover himself. I went to Mexico and discovered Rivera *and* myself."

In 1971 Gorman noted: "I'm often compared to Orozco and other Mexican artists like Raul Anguiano and Zuñiga. I'm always flattered by the comparison. We are depicting the same thing, so why shouldn't there be a similarity?"

In his drawings, Gorman is more often compared to Francisco Zuñiga than any of the others. Like Zuñiga, Gorman's favorite subjects in the medium are women, large monumental women. Zuñiga extended this preference to his sculpture; in fact, many of his drawings were preliminary sketches for sculptures. In the book, *Zuñiga,* author Ali Chumacero describes Zuñiga's drawings. With the exception of locale, it could also serve as a description of Gorman's current drawings and lithographs:

> . . . Zuñiga has persisted in finding in the men and women of the southeastern part of Mexico, themes which inspire his sensibilities. But though he has situated these figures in a realistic context he has not let himself be carried away by the temptation toward the picturesque. On the contrary, his purpose is quite different: his people, inhabitants of a highly individualized part of the country, are perceived at the doorways of their huts, in the marketplace or strolling along the streets, and he transports them to a different level, leading them toward a life that, without weakening the ties which their geographical origin bestows on them, transforms them into creatures who are masters of their own reality.[16]

One senses that Gorman and Zuñiga may start from the same premise, the same emotional responses, the same predilections, but at the moment the pencil or crayon touches the paper the dichotomy begins. Zuñiga utilizes many more lines in depicting his figures, more facial detail, more shading of bodies and garments. This is more apparent in Gorman's early drawings. In recent years Gorman has been shedding all but basic lines, moving toward large, loose renderings of the figure, with a minimum of detail and shading.

Still, if one were asked to select the Mexican master in the medium of drawing whose work might be most aptly compared with Gorman's, it would be Zuñiga. And for color, Tamayo. His influence would appear in Gorman's paintings some ten years later.

Gorman had been doing the human figure long before he went to Mexico (witness his early childhood efforts), but in Mexico his interest and competence in delineating

9

the figure were both encouraged and intensified. "My style evolved there — my graphics, my people. At Mexico City College we did the basic things first — nudes, lots of them. Then when I came back to the reservation, that wasn't so easy to come by — nude models, I mean — so I started doing women with clothes on, and that," he adds, laughing, "seems to have paid off in its way.

"When I came back from Mexico, I went through my blue period, just like Picasso. I went through a lot of other periods, too, but they came later, in San Francisco."

Gorman did not stay on the reservation long. In 1962 he left for San Francisco, vowing that he would never live in a hogan again. The first several months in the big city were not easy for a poor artist. "I was desperate. Finally I got a job at the post office and worked there all night and painted all day. I can't believe now I had all that energy, but I was young. I took a few art courses at San Francisco State College and later I worked as a model there and at other colleges and private art studios in the area. I was very sought after as a model. Not only did it pay, I learned while I was being paid!"

Gorman had said, "The navy was my first introduction to the outside world." He did not know then that this world would claim him. He returned to the reservation often, but he never returned to the Navajo Way again. Yet, his Navajo heritage, the mixed collection of childhood experiences and impressions, became his most essential luggage. He would carry it with him everywhere.

RECOGNITION AND RETURN 1963–1970

BY 1963 Gorman had put in seven years of intensive application to his art. Many of his works had sold, but he was not widely known. In Mexico he had discovered himself as an artist; during his first year in San Francisco he had added to his training. Now he was ready to receive broader exposure, to enlarge his horizons. If he had planned it, he could not have chosen a better time. The art world was just beginning to recognize that there were a number of individual Indian artists who could make vital contributions to the mainstream of American art. The Southwest Indian Art project sponsored by the Rockefeller Foundation at the University of Arizona, Tucson, during the summers of 1960, 1961, and 1962, had shaken off the lethargy into which Indian arts had fallen. It shaped the philosophy of the Institute of American Indian Arts, established by the Bureau of Indian Affairs in 1962. It also influenced the policy of the Scottsdale National Indian Arts Council which held the first of its exhibitions in 1961. By 1970 its standards would include: "... honoring the avant-garde as well as the traditional ... to recognize that today's Indian artists cannot be stereotyped ... to recognize the rights of Indian artists to experiment, to use new media and new technology, to evolve in their artistic expressions as any other artist."[17]

This was, indeed, an ideal climate for the nurture and flowering of Gorman's art. The first showing of his work in San Francisco was at the Zieniewicz Gallery. Later in 1963, he had a one-man show at the Coffee Gallery. Artist Cynthia Bissell recalls the first time she met Gorman. "I had just come back to San Francisco after having lived on the Navajo Reservation, and I was very much involved with Indian art. When I read in the paper that a Navajo artist was showing at the Coffee Gallery, of course I went. At the time Gorman was doing a lot of things directly from the Navajo country. There was one painting in the show I've never forgotten, *Spider Woman*. I was very impressed with his work, perhaps most of all, that it was an Indian doing it, that he wasn't doing it like Mr. Yazz or the other Indian painters I had seen. After that we met on and off at parties, and whenever he had shows I went to them."

Gorman's colorful personality and appearance, his unique art could not go unnoticed long, even in such a large and sophisticated city as San Francisco. He was becoming known in the area and having an increasing number of shows. He also had the good fortune to have as his patrons Charles and Ruth de Young Elkus, who had contributed so much to the recognition of Indian art through the encouragement of young artists, as well as assembling one of the major collections of Indian art in the country.

For Gorman it was a time for refining techniques and exploring new styles. "I was going through a lot of different periods. After Mexico, it was the blue period and then a surrealism period. That was actually a surrealistic approach to my own self. Unfortunately, all of the works I did then were either sold, or I gave them away or destroyed them."

In the summer of 1964, Gorman made a trip to the Southwest and stopped in Taos, New Mexico. "There I met a friendly sculptor named Frank Lyon who suggested I move to Taos. First, he said, I should visit all the galleries, especially the Manchester Gallery." This was a picturesque old adobe complex on Ledoux Street. It was said that parts of the present structure had been built over two hundred years ago by the Indians of Taos Pueblo. In the 1920s it had been purchased by Eleanora Kissel, an artist from New York, as a place to live in and paint during the summers. She did portraits of many of the citizens of Taos, including one of the noted artist, Dorothy Brett. This is now in the Harwood Foundation, just down the street from the gallery. In 1962, John Manchester had purchased the property adjacent to it, and in 1963 he purchased the old adobe building from Eleanora Kissel, and opened the Manchester Gallery there on Christmas Eve, 1963.[18]

The buildings and the man Gorman was about to meet there were to have a profound effect on his career and his lifestyle. John Manchester recalls the event: "I was sitting back in the office when Gorman walked into the gallery with Barry Tinkler (a Houston artist). They looked around for quite some time. Then my assistant in the gallery came back to the office and said, 'There's an Indian boy here who wants you to see slides of his paintings.' I told him to look at them and if he liked them to let me take a look. Shortly after, he came back and said he thought they were exciting. The minute I started looking through the slides — well, by about the second painting I would have bought them all. We sat and talked to Gorman for a while. He had been told to see another gallery first and would not commit himself. I told him that if he decided he wanted me to show his work, I couldn't promise him a one-man show until next year, but that I would like to have a few things as soon as possible, begin talking about him, get interest going before we did a big show. He said, 'Fine,' he would think about it. Well, he wrote me a very amusing letter saying that he had looked at all the galleries in Taos and that he would rather be part of a *smorgasbord* than to be in a supermarket, and therefore he had decided to show with me. Shortly after that I received two or three paintings. Then he started sending me more and more, writing me every week. Then he came to visit and stayed here at the house and we got to know each other better. He did a wonderful portrait of Brett [Dorothy Brett] during that visit.

"We had done some publicity and advertising and sold a number of his paintings already, so we planned a one-man show for our best season, September. Gorman was sending more and more paintings and I filled the large room with them as well as the glass cases in front. I changed the décor — added some Indian motifs to complement his work.

"It was one of the most exciting shows I've ever seen, and people in town said, 'This is the way openings used to be years ago.' I had Gorman's mother and Aunt Mary staying here at the house. His father and stepmother were in town for the opening. People came from all over. I brought in a group of Indian friends from Taos Pueblo and they did a series of dances, and later everyone joined in the Friendship Dance or Circle Dance.

"This was Gorman's first one-man show in the Southwest and it was a tremendous success. I will have to say, Gorman is his own best salesman — he's so completely open and he was bubbling all day, talking with everyone, and his father being there and his mother — it created an atmosphere — well, I don't know how to describe it, except that I've never had an opening like it, and I've never been to one since that was quite as beautiful an amalgamation of Anglo and Indian. People I would never have expected to buy paintings bought them. People I would never have expected to be so excited were. It was almost like a new beginning, a revolution of some kind.

"It established a new relationship for the gallery in the direction of Indian things. Up until this point no Indian paintings had been shown anywhere in the area, except the traditional old-style paintings and these were shown mostly in Indian shops and gift shops, not in art galleries. Many people at the show said Gorman was by far the foremost of the young Indian painters, but as we kept telling everyone: 'Don't call him an Indian painter. He is a painter first and foremost. He happens to paint Indian things because this is the way of life he has lived.' To call him an 'Indian painter' in the old sense of the word just didn't fit at all.

"I think every Indian painter in the modern school who has made it since was helped by Gorman and was influenced by him. I've always thought he was the forerunner of the whole movement. When you consider that when we started with Gorman, the Institute of American Indian Art in Santa Fe was just barely beginning. *Bury My Heart at Wounded Knee* hadn't even been published. None of the other revolutionary-style books had been written. Fritz Scholder had not yet started his Indian series. I can't think of anything that was happening when we started with Gorman that could have had a greater influence on young Indian artists searching for their independence.

"After that one-man show Gorman would come every year and spend two days to a week. Of course, we did very well with his work and continued to do very well."

After his successful Taos show, Gorman returned to San Francisco and proceeded with another new style he had recently developed. "I went through a landscape period. Well, actually I integrated the landscape and the people so that they almost became one. One of the preliminary sketches I did for a painting in this period is in an old notebook of mine. It shows two women standing together; one is holding a baby, and then the landscape zipping through, and yet, they are part of it, integrated with it." The painting referred to may be *Two Navajo Women and Child,* one of several paintings by Indian artists used to illustrate articles by Jeanne O. Snodgrass and Dorothy Dunn in the Winter, 1965, issue of *Western Review.* The painting is bold and dramatic, very different from any of Gorman's other mother-and-child themes, and gives exactly the effect he described when discussing his landscape period. In her article, Jeanne Snodgrass makes the following comment on Gorman: "For some artists the phase of 'traditional' painting existed only a short while or not at all: Fritz Scholder, Adele Collins, and R. C. Gorman, for instance, were 'non-traditionalists' from the start. Characteristic of their outlook is a statement made recently by R. C. Gorman: 'I see no progress in traditional anything. . . . I have not strayed, really . . . merely improvised . . . The reservation is my source of inspiration. . . .' "[19]

One of the paintings used to illustrate the articles was done by Carl Gorman. The previous year (1964) he and R. C. had their first father-and-son show at the Philbrook Museum and Art Center in Tulsa and in 1965, at the Heard Museum in Phoenix.

In 1966, Gorman helped organize the American Indian Artists group in San Francisco, and served as chairman of its painting committee. Another Southwest Indian artist who was active in the group was Swazo Hinds of Tesuque Pueblo, New Mexico. The group was mentioned by Dorothy Dunn in a 1972 article in *Plateau:* "In January 1971, painters of this group, and former associates, initiated and staged on their own a full-fledged exhibition in the new Oakland

Museum. This show encompassed all stages and several tribal representatives of the modern school, from Soqween and Beatien Yazz to Swazo, Gorman, Earl Livermore, Woesha Cloud North, Peter Blue Cloud, and others who are becoming known in the Bay Area."[20] Gorman had two one-man shows in San Francisco in 1966 and one of his drawings, a Navajo woman grinding corn, was featured in the painting section of Tom Bahti's book, *Southwestern Indian Arts and Crafts*.

Meanwhile Gorman was immersed in yet another period: "During my surrealism period, I was working in oil, but then I switched to acrylics. I can't handle them the same way. When you work with oil, it's smooth, like cream; you tell it what to do, you manipulate it, whereas acrylic has a mind of its own, so I developed an entirely new approach to handling these colors. First I did the impasto technique and then a very watery approach. Finally, I developed this binding of color bits, and from that approach I developed my rug series. After that came the pottery series. There I used the same technique, only I aged it a little more — by hosing, throwing buckets of water at it, and by tossing sand on it. As I experimented with acrylics different techniques evolved themselves, and I guess as far as subject matter goes, I was being drawn back to the things that impressed me at home — rug weaving, pottery motifs."

These two series proved to be among his most popular and distinctive paintings. Some of them were first shown at his one-man show at the Heard Museum in 1967.

It was around this time that Gorman met Father Wilfred Schoenberg, who was to become a close and long-time friend. They met while Father Schoenberg was in San Francisco purchasing paintings for his museum, Pacific Northwest Indian Center, at Gonzaga University in Spokane, Washington. Father Schoenberg recalls visiting Gorman's San Francisco studio: "R. C. lived in the Upper Market area, on Army Street. It was up on a hill, at least ten flights up. He had all sorts of pots, lots of cats, and a beautiful view, but R. C. told me he didn't like San Francisco at all. I remember a huge painting I got from him on that visit. It was eight feet high by four feet wide. We had to take it out of the stretcher to get it home. It was the first painting in that particular style that he had ever done. It had six or seven large horse skulls against a Navajo blanket pattern, big dripping globs of red, a violent red. It's an angry painting in a way; yet, I've never seen R. C. angry. When I asked him about it, he said he had been in a mood the day he painted it. He said: 'I *was* angry.' The painting was shown at the Unitarian Church in San Francisco and was there for quite a while. At that time, I remember, he had an apartment full of triptychs, his pottery motifs. They were very nice. Then he did a series of works that were all very sad — ten in a row — and I asked him, 'Why are you so sad, so depressed in this art?' R. C. told me, 'My father had an automobile accident and his son [Gorman's half-brother] was killed. While my father was in the hospital, I did a portrait of him and that was sad. I started doing some sad paintings then.' "

Carl Gorman wrote of this accident in 1974 when he was director of Native Healing Sciences for the Navajo Health Authority. He tells of the bone injuries he received in August, 1966. "The doctors told me I would never walk again without crutches . . . In November I was shoveling snow and the X-rays showed no trace of where the traction pins had been."[21] The summer following the accident (1967) he and R. C. had a father-and-son show, presented by the American Indian Historical Society in San Francisco.

During the 1960s Gorman had been entering Indian exhibitions throughout the West. This brought him to the attention of another person who would be influential in his future career. Dr. Byron C. Butler of Phoenix notes: "I had been collecting Indian art for some time, and I was very impressed with the works of Gorman I had seen at the Scottsdale National and other shows. We went to San Francisco especially to meet him. I remember we had some trouble finding his apartment, and when we did, we climbed five flights of stairs, only to be met with a sign on the door: 'To Whom It May Concern: I am in the little brown house on the top of the hill. Love, R. C. Gorman.' We then had to go back down the steps, get in the car and drive around the block and climb about twenty more flights of stairs. There was Gorman at last, sitting very happily drinking wine with some artist friends. At that time he was doing geometric abstract paintings and drawings of Navajo women. The drawings were similar to those he is doing now, but more detailed. We purchased two or three paintings and later took him to dinner at a French restaurant. That was the beginning of our long association."

It was during this period, when Gorman was doing more detailed drawings, that the Navajo celebrated the one hundredth anniversary of their return to their homeland following the Treaty of 1868. On the somber side, it was also an observance of the four years of exile and imprisonment at Bosque Redondo and the miseries of the "round-up" and The Long Walk. The drawings Gorman did in 1968 commemorating this tragic event come closer than any work he has done before or since to making a political comment. Perhaps he was remembering his great-grandfather. Though Peshlakai died before Gorman was born, it is likely that Carl Gorman had heard his story often and passed it on to his son. The impact of the event on the Navajo is described by Dr. Salsbury in his account of the years spent at Ganado Mission: "When I arrived in 1927, the treaty was only fifty-nine years old. There were elders who remembered The Long Walk and a sad childhood at Bosque Redondo. Middle-aged people had heard the story so often that they felt it as a personal experience. Only the young were reasonably free of historic bitterness."[22]

In these studies, Gorman used many fine lines to delineate facial expressions that testified to grief, desperation and despair. Clara Lee Tanner notes: "In his Long Walk subjects he had full opportunity to portray starvation in big deep eyes, the aged, bent figures, the anguished postures of fatigued bodies, the gaunt faces and boney hands, suffering bare feet."[23] This was a different side of Gorman and evidences his capacity to express great depth of feeling. It was, perhaps, this series which led critics to compare him to Käthe Kollwitz, the German Expressionist who portrayed people in anguish in numerous etchings, woodcuts, and lithographs, which art historian John Canaday places "among the most vigorous graphic productions of the early twentieth century."[24]

John Manchester once commented: "I think Gorman is painting the beautiful essence of the Indian. I think there's nothing more beautiful than some of his Indian Madonnas. I feel he is painting an Indian essence which comes out of himself."

Not everyone, however, was in agreement as to how that "Indian essence" should be expressed. Despite the more liberal policies established by the Southwest Indian Art Project in the early 1960s, there were still many traditionalists among Indian art experts and collectors who did not want to see Indian painting change from the pattern it had followed for over half a century.

Gorman met Dorothy Dunn, whose name had become synonymous with traditional Indian painting, sometime after the publication of her 1968 book, *American Indian Painting*, and they got along famously. Later he had this comment to make on the artists who had studied under her at the Santa Fe Indian School's studio in the 1930s: "I think it was a very important evolutionary movement for the Indian painters. Unfortunately, some young painters today think that's *it* and they continue painting in the same way. That's the only objection I have. But I think she really made a huge and lasting contribution to the forming of Indian painters. They had to start somewhere, and her studio was the beginning of formalized Indian painting."

The 1960s had been an important decade for Gorman. He had established a niche for himself in the art world; he had met a number of people who would be important in his future life and career. One of the most important events took place near the end of the decade: in 1968 Gorman had another one-man exhibit at the Manchester Gallery in Taos, one of many he had had there since his first successful show in 1965. The old adobe buildings, the handsome spacious gallery had pleasant associations for him, and in 1968, he purchased it from Manchester. It would now be known as the Navajo Gallery and would also be his home and studio for many years to come. In a 1971 interview with Robert A. Ewing at the gallery, he said: "I had my first one-man show in Taos, in this house, which was then owned by John Manchester. I just walked in and showed him some of my work and he arranged the show. He wouldn't like me to say this, but he has been like a guiding father to me."[25]

Gorman was happily settled in his studio-home-gallery complex by 1969 when Cynthia Bissell came to Taos. She recalls: "I came here just for a visit, but after I had looked around I thought, 'Good grief! I don't want to go back to San Francisco!' So I told Gorman that I was simply going to go back and pick up my stuff and move to New Mexico. About a week later Gorman called me and said, 'Why don't you come right now? I've found you a house.' So I came."

"Cynthia has been a very important part of my life," Gorman said. She was one of many artists whose works would be exhibited regularly at the Navajo Gallery. Another friend from Gorman's San Francisco days to exhibit frequently at the gallery was Swazo Hinds. He, too, had returned to the Southwest (in 1969), settling in Santa Fe, just a few miles from his native pueblo, Tesuque. Gorman's presence in Taos also drew many of his collectors there for the first time.

In 1969 Gorman entered the Scottsdale National Indian Arts Exhibition and wound up the decade with a flourish by taking three awards. One of his Navajo rug paintings and an abstract took first and third awards, while a drawing took second.

Though Gorman was rapidly becoming established as one of the major Southwest Indian artists, he said he didn't know if he had made any impact on his own people: "I may be a prophet without honor in my own country."

This was disputed by Virginia Dooley, who was teaching on the reservation in the late 1960s: "I had never met R. C. but I remember when he opened the gallery, it was written up in the *Navajo Times* and everybody thought it was fantastic. It was *the* topic of conversation, where I lived at any rate, at Window Rock and Fort Defiance. No other Indian had ever done this before. It was a real source of pride to the Navajos. I used to hang prints of Gorman's paintings up on the bulletin board in my classroom. I had one student, Harrison Begay [not the famous Indian painter], and he was a very talented artist. When I asked him what he was going to do when he graduated, he said, 'I'm going to paint. I've already sold some of my things and someday I'll be good enough to show my paintings in the Navajo Gallery.' " As it turned out it was Virginia, herself, who was to become involved in the gallery. She became its director in 1973.

NEW MEDIUMS — NEW HORIZONS 1970–1976

MEXICO CITY, which had been the birthplace of Gorman's new directions in drawing and painting, was also the starting point for another major development in his career. For some time he had been searching for a graphic medium which would allow him to duplicate his drawings without loss of quality. His intention was to make them available to a broader spectrum of the public. He had done woodcuts and linoleum block prints in the past, but neither of these was suitable for duplicating his present style of drawing.

Thus when Raul Anguiano, during a chance meeting in Scottsdale in 1966, suggested he try lithography and recommended his own lithographer, José Sanchez in Mexico City, Gorman acted upon the suggestion immediately. He made several trips to Mexico City, and by 1970 had completed five lithographs under Sanchez's tutelage. It was a good place to begin. Mexico had a long tradition in the graphic arts, and José Sanchez had printed for most of the major artists of Mexico at the Taller de Gráfica Popular in Mexico City. Dr. Jules Heller, who printed there as visiting artist in the summer of 1947, remembers Sanchez and notes that many American artists flocked to the Taller during the 1940s to work in the lithographic medium. As Garo Antreasian and Clinton Adams observed in *The Tamarind Book of Lithography:* "By 1960, lithographic workshops had all but disappeared in this country. There were few master printers, and it was only with the greatest difficulty that an artist might engage himself in lithography. As a result, few of the major artists working in the United States made lithographs during the 1940s and 1950s."[26] It was not until 1960, when the Tamarind Lithography Workshop, under the direction of June Wayne, was established in Los Angeles, that the art began to revive in this country.

The lithographs Gorman completed in Mexico were shown in his Navajo Gallery and appeared in several of his shows. *Three Taos Men,* especially, received much attention and was later featured in *Southwest Indian Painting* (1973). But the five works he had completed in Mexico were not enough to establish him in the lithographic field.

Since Gorman's return to the Southwest, Dr. Byron C. Butler, who had gone to San Francisco especially to meet him in the late 1960s, continued to show an interest in his work and became a major patron. Butler suggested the idea of forming a partnership with him to do suites of lithographs, and in the fall of 1971 Gorman began working on his first lithographs in this country at the Tamarind Institute, newly located at the University of New Mexico in Albuquerque. The result was a suite of five lithographs titled *Homage to Navajo Women.* This, along with several individual lithographs, was presented to the public at a preview party in March, 1972. They had an enthusiastic reception and were purchased for the permanent collections of several major museums. The lithographic medium proved ideal for Gorman's talents and for his original intention of reaching a broader spectrum of the public. In collaboration with Dr. Butler and Tamarind Institute, he produced five suites and eight individual lithographs between 1971 and 1974.

In 1971 Gorman completed a major painting. Through his association with Dr. Butler, he was commissioned by Saint Luke's Hospital in Phoenix to do a large mural. Titled *Hohokam Masked Dancers,* it is an acrylic on canvas and measures 110 by 75 inches. The deity figures it portrays and its colors of red and buff were copied from a piece of pottery dated around A.D. 900 which had been found at Saint Luke's site during the Snaketown Excavation conducted by the University of Arizona's archaeology depart-

ment. The mural is in the main reception area of the hospital. A bronze plaque next to it bears its legend and Gorman's name. Several years later, Gorman mentioned the painting when asked what he hoped to convey through his work. "I think everything I paint should have a personal appeal to the viewer. I want it to be looked at and appreciated differently by different people. I do that myself. My appreciation for my art changes from year to year. Every time I see the mural at Saint Luke's, I really like it better. It was so huge, I had to have three people help me move it up and down. I had a lot of help on that — from Virginia Dooley, Curtis Grubbs, and then Anton Balcomb made special stretcher bars for it. I had all of them put their names on the back of it."

Gorman had a number of important shows in the early 1970s, including several two-man shows in California, New Mexico, and Indiana, and one-man shows in Texas, Arizona, New Mexico, and Colorado, as well as group exhibitions throughout the country. In 1970 he crisscrossed the United States six times — once he flew from New York to San Francisco "just to ride a 747." He was also producing shows at his Navajo Gallery for other artists: in addition to Swazo Hinds and Cynthia Bissell, shows for his father, Charles Lovato, Jerry Ingram, Tony Da, Clifford Beck, Tony Begay, Dan Namingha; and Anglo artists such as Tavlos, Constance Counter, Ann Moule, and Frank Lyon, the sculptor who had first suggested Gorman move to Taos. By 1974 he had exhibited the works of some seventy artists at his gallery. Some were well known, for others it provided the first major showing of their works and was the stepping-stone to greater recognition. Gorman was proud of the artists he exhibited and took great pride in the singular claim: "I'm the only Navajo in the country to own my own gallery." The business aspects of it were another thing: "I'm also the worst businessman in the world, that's for sure, but I have so many people helping me."

While in the 1960s the recognition of Indian artists was gradually accelerating, in the 1970s it exploded, and the hub of the activity was in the Southwest. From there it radiated out to the rest of the country. Scottsdale and Santa Fe were the major art centers and, largely due to Gorman's Navajo Gallery, Taos was also attracting considerable attention in the field.

In her 1973 book, Clara Lee Tanner wrote: "R. C. Gorman is one of the most dynamic of the young artists who became well known in the 1960s and who moved steadily toward non-Indian art techniques."[27]

Gorman was continuing with his Navajo rug and pottery motifs in his painting. These were enormously successful, and he did infinite variations on the themes and often developed unusual ways of handling the canvas. In 1971 Joan Bucklew, art critic for the *Arizona Republic,* reviewed one of his current shows: "Bleeding abstractions in many soft corrosive layers of polymer on canvas may suggest time-mellowed rug or pottery motifs. Sometimes a triptych, or even polyptych, is made of separate modular canvases to be juxtaposed as one chooses. *The Manta*, in three parts, spans the height of a wall and turns the corner at the ceiling, while another work in five sections turns a corner of the exhibit room."[28]

Gorman's observations on the themes were: "I have been using the design motifs of Indian rugs and pottery for my paintings because one day these things are going to be no more. They are going to be lost, and it is going to happen soon. It will be a white America by A.D. 2000. The Indian art that people are enjoying now — the rugs and pottery — are no longer going to be there. It's inevitable: complete integration. I am amused that I sell my rug paintings for more than the actual rug sells for; perhaps the paintings are worth more in the long run. Moths don't like polymers."

The other facet of his work was described in the 1971 Bucklew review: "There is a sampling of lithography; understated drawings in charcoal and pastel; lots bright with color. Wetting a charcoal pastel and giving it a watercolor-wash treatment is a Gorman trademark. Navajo women, nude or clothed, are the subjects viewers look forward to season after season."[29]

This was true then as it is today. Collectors could not seem to get enough of his women. One collector noted recently: "Gorman's women are pleasant to live with. They wear well." Their figures were fuller than is considered fashionable today, but Gorman explained: "I choose models who have full bodies — something you can put your two arms around and feel a real woman. I like the ample figure because it fills space softly."

In 1974, art critic Dr. Harry Wood noted: "Gorman's women wear their blankets like the spotless chasubles of priestesses." And later: "In the bound black hair, he discovers an infinite alphabet of shapes. Only the Japanese have known how to make a bundle of black hair the key that locks together a whole drawing. There is a grace in these mighty women. . . ."[30]

Another quality which brought collectors back year after year, even those who already had an extensive collection of Gorman women, was a fact singled out by Dr. Wood: "He works only from live models . . . and though he has done thousands of drawings, he never repeats a pose or a gesture."

Gorman also had something to say about his models: "It's a necessity for me to work from a live model — the rapport we establish creates a sort of psychic energy. We may not say much, but there are vibrations and they set the mood for the drawing. If she is down, depressed, it comes through; if she is happy, or relaxed, then that comes through in the drawing."

Edmond Gaultney, who was Gorman's gallery director in 1971, observed: "His model has to be natural, and the women he likes best are women that are close to the earth. He likes mothers, and sometimes his models will bring their children." Commenting on Gorman's working methods, he said: "When he paints he throws the water and the paint on the canvas in dancelike movements. He can't rework them; the same with his drawings. When he has to labor over a drawing it's not going to be good. It only takes him ten minutes to do a very fine drawing, his best work. He may go back thirty minutes later or the next day and add a brushstroke here or there, but basically what happens, happens in ten minutes."

Gorman notes that "I don't *attack* the canvas. I just throw paint on the canvas and there it is. It should be such that it frightens *me*, not me frightening my canvas."

By the mid-1970s more and more critics were using the word "universal" when describing his work. A Chicago reviewer noted: "While Gorman's subject matter is derived from his Navajo heritage, it clearly transcends that. There is a universality in his work."[31]

Throughout the time of social unrest that marked the 1960s and early 1970s, Gorman never joined any Indian activist groups. Edmond Gaultney noted: "Gorman has no political concept; in fact, I think politics bores him. But I have seen him become very angry at some people's attitudes toward Indians or if he sees Indians mistreated. Then, I have seen him take action. He doesn't expound on his political beliefs, but when the occasion arises, he seizes the moment and acts."

Gorman himself said: "I'm not politically inclined — toward 'Red Power,' that sort of thing. I don't really consider myself different. I'm Indian, yes, but the only time I realize I am is when I'm told I am. I see myself first of all as an artist. Yet, on the other hand, I'm very proud of the fact that I'm an Indian with a certain amount of ability."

In his own way, Gorman was helping the Indian — by sponsoring Indian artists, exhibiting their works at his gallery and by his own work. He did, as John Manchester noted, "portray the beautiful essence of the Indian. He portrays the Indian as he likes to see himself."

During the early 1970s, Gorman was not only establishing a wide following in the West, but was becoming nationally known. Visitors to the Southwest were buying his works and carrying them back to their homes in every part of the country. His works could be found in the private collections of many notable persons, from movie stars to industrialists and statesmen, as well as major museum collections.

In 1973 he was singled out for a major honor when he was the only living American Indian artist to be included in the show, *Masterworks of the Museum of the American Indian*, which was held at the Metropolitan Museum of Art in New York. In addition, two of his drawings were selected for the cover of the exhibit's catalog. He also has the distinction of being the only living Indian artist to be included in the Metropolitan Museum's permanent collection. In 1974 his abilities as a writer were brought before the public when a short story of his was included in *The*

Man to Send Rain Clouds, an anthology edited by Kenneth Rosen and published by Viking Press. He and Aaron Yava also co-illustrated the book.

Early in 1975 he was selected for another singular honor: a one-man exhibit at the Museum of the American Indian, Heye Foundation, New York City. It was distinguished as "the first in a series of one-man exhibitions of the work of contemporary Indian artists, in an effort to further demonstrate the wealth of creativity which is alive and active in the field of Native American Art, and as a measure of the success of Indian artists in today's world."[32] The members' preview of the Gorman exhibition as reported by director Frederick J. Dockstader, had "attracted the largest single group for an opening of this nature that we have enjoyed to date."[33]

Later in 1975 he was one of seventeen southwestern contemporary artists and craftsmen included in the book, *Art and Indian Individualists.* In the same year, he was one of seven artists selected for the *American Indian Artists* film series produced by the Public Broadcasting Service's station KAET/Phoenix. The film *R. C. Gorman* was narrated by Rod McKuen and, along with the rest of the series, received national airing over Public Broadcasting Service stations in August, 1976.

Thus, in the first half of the 1970s, R. C. Gorman had established himself as a gallery owner, entrepreneur for some seventy other artists, and a nationally known figure in the art world, represented in major shows, books, articles, and a film. Through all of this he was producing — paintings and drawings plus over sixty works in his new medium of lithography.

By the end of 1975, when asked what the highpoints in his life were, he could say: "I've had so many highpoints that to go over them individually would take all day, and I really hate to bore anyone."

NEW MEDIUMS — NEW HORIZONS 1976–1978

DURING 1976 AND 1977, Gorman went into a frenzy of activity going in many directions at once. Though the 1970s had been good to him professionally, he had suffered a series of blows in his personal life. Between 1972 and 1975 he lost his mother, his half-brother, Douglas, and his good friend Patrick Swazo Hinds. In March of 1976, his uncle, John Day, from Canyon de Chelly died; within days, another half-brother, Butch, died, and several days after that his uncle, Steve Gorman, was killed. Gorman was constantly called out on some serious family crisis. In addition to this, his own health was precarious. Gorman will share his successes, happy moments, laughter with everyone, but he keeps any serious personal problems to himself. In regard to the losses of so many who had been close to him, his cousin Grace notes: "He never talks about it. He is a very private person. He reads a great deal and is subject to melancholia and serious reflection, but has a great capac-

ity in his inner self. Of all my relatives I feel closest to him. I find his outlook on life enjoyable. He doesn't brood about the past. He's future oriented."

It was, perhaps, this determination to look ahead which drove Gorman in 1976 and 1977. Despite deep personal distress, at the end of these two years he had completed works in seven different mediums, four of them completely new to him.

In 1976, in addition to preparing works for four major shows in Chicago, Wichita, New Orleans, and Santa Fe, and the production of twenty lithographs, he began work in a new medium — etching. In mid-July he went to Hand Graphics, Ltd., in Santa Fe where his *Enigma* suite of lithographs had been printed earlier in the year. Working with printer Ron Adams, he executed his first etching — a study of a seated Navajo woman. This was printed in three states of varying colors, a complex and ambitious effort for a first try. By early 1978 he had completed five others done in a single color, either burnt umber or burnt sienna. He commented that he was rather "lukewarm" about etching at first. "I, personally, feel that I didn't get that much involved because I did not feel I could control my line. It requires a completely different line than any other medium I've worked in. It's not like the Gorman line." The problem he had with the medium is understandable: in his drawings and lithographs he is used to the broad sweeping line, usually on a large surface. He notes that he prefers to work on large stones in his lithographic production. The image size in the last five etchings is considerably smaller, approximately eight by ten inches. One could say that the medium literally "cramps his style." Yet, several of these first etchings have a richness in depth and contrast which indicates his potential in the medium.

In 1977 he accelerated his productivity still more. In addition to his etchings, the execution of some two dozen lithographs, as well as drawings and paintings for nine major shows across the country from California to New York, he began work in three other mediums: silk-screening, sculpture, and ceramics.

His first venture into silk-screening took place at Serigraphics in Albuquerque, working with Harry Westlund, who had printed many of his early lithographs at Tamarind. Here again his efforts were ambitious for firsts in a new medium — all are done in five or six colors. Due to the technical demands of the medium, his favorite subjects, Navajo women, have a different look: their faces are more crisply delineated and their patterned shawls, done in striking summer awning colors, stand out from the landscape like bright umbrellas on a beach. One exception is a woman's head rendered in very pale pastels, suggesting the variety he can achieve. Five of his serigraphs were exhibited in his February, 1978, show. One of them, *The Gossips,* was also adapted in a large seven-by-five-foot tapestry, the first time any of his works have been adapted to such a medium.

It was Walter Maibaum of Editions Press in San Francisco, where a number of Gorman's lithographs had been printed in the past two years, who urged Gorman to try sculpture. It had been many years since Gorman did his first sculptures in the mud of Chinle Wash, and he was reluctant. Maibaum says, "It took a long time to convince him to try a sculpture. One night I sat alone in my shop and molded in clay, using one of the women in his lithographs as a model. I had never sculpted before, but I managed a reasonable facsimile. The next morning I showed it to R. C. and he was surprised. I said, 'Now if I can do it, you can.' This convinced him and he began work. He likes to use one of our women printers, Evelyn Lincoln, as his model. The first sculpture he completed is *Seated Woman*." This was followed by four other studies of women ranging in size from twelve to twenty-four inches high. All were cast in bronze and published by Editions Press in editions of ten. One of them, a woman's head, is titled *Angelina*, the name of one of Gorman's favorite models who has appeared often in both his drawings and lithographs. Her long turquoise hishi earrings were made by Gorman's friend, Santo Domingo artist Charles Lovato. By the time he had completed the five sculptures Gorman had gained so much confidence that he did a larger-than-life-size figure of a seated woman (five-and-one-half-feet high). This was cast in bronze in April 1978, and published in an edition of six. The work reveals how easily his interpretations of women can be translated into the monumental. In late April, Gorman was again in San Francisco to begin a different work in the medium — a bust of his father. Carl Gorman had flown over with him to model for it. The *Today Show* filmed the father-son team at work. Once having gotten over his initial reluctance, this is a medium Gorman finds very satisfying. The transition from drawing to sculpture is a natural one, as drawing is an essential prelude to the medium. One is again reminded of Zuñiga, with whom Gorman has so often been compared in the graphic arts. Ali Chumacero observes in the book *Zuñiga:* "He soon abandoned painting . . . to concentrate his energies in sculpture, and at the same time, often as preliminary sketches for a sculptured work, he practiced drawing. These two are the twin phases of the artistic work of Francisco Zuñiga, the paths along which his talents have taken him."[34]

During 1977 Gorman was making another approach to clay — ceramics. For this he was working under the tutelage of potter Maxine Guy of Tubac, Arizona. "I was pretty discouraged about my progress and probably won't do more until I can give it more time." He did, however, decorate a number of jugs, platters, and pitchers, working in conjunction with Tubac potter Tom Forgey. Seven of these were featured in his February show. Most were quite large and featured deep bronzed or black nude figures, male and female, on pale, putty-colored clay. One, a twenty-inch-high jug, featured his mother-and-child theme, with the sienna-colored figures and the inner lip of the jug accented in brilliant blue. The pieces are handsome and distinctive; some, such as the *He-She Pitcher Pair*, are typical of the Gorman whimsy. His painted forms adapt surprisingly well to the rounded surfaces.

Among the sixty-five works in his February show, twenty-nine were devoted to oil pastel drawings, thirteen to lithographs, only two to painting, and the balance divided about evenly between his four new mediums. Whether this is indicative of the ratio for future shows is unpredictable. Gorman might very well surprise his followers with yet another medium, or become engrossed in one to the exclusion of several others.

One would think that any artist with such a back-breaking schedule and diversity of mediums would be working at least eighteen hour a day under nerve-wracking pressure. Not so. Gorman never allows work to interfere with pleasure. More often than not, he combines them. Ben Q. Adams, who has printed Gorman's lithographs for six years — from the early Tamarind days — provides a capsule version of Gorman's modus operandi while working on lithographs at Western Graphics: "When R. C. arrives at the workshop (at 8:00 or 8:30 A.M) the atmosphere is immediately changed, and all of the activities of the shop, for the most part, revolve around him. Because of the speed with which he works, he demands constant attention, and new stones and plates are prepared while he works on the key image. He is constantly joking and has many things on his mind. While he is drawing he is often concerned about his Mercedes, whether it needs to be washed or needs some minor repair. He also likes to think about some gourmet food or Japanese food, which my wife, Yoko, often prepares for him. There is always the entourage of people who want to see him for some reason or other, and questions from those who work for him about some decision that has to be made. He likes to dance around the shop to Spanish music, so we have the radio tuned into a Spanish station for him. He will usually spend the morning, until 11:30, working off and on on the stone, and joking, talking on the phone, and in general just having a good time. He usually does not return to the workshop until 2:00 P.M. (after a gourmet lunch with wine). He will work an hour or an hour and a half after lunch, and then will disappear until the next morning." (One suspects the afternoon nap here, the childhood habit he would not give up even on the first day of school.) Adams adds: "I am usually exhausted after working with him, as his energy never stops. I might also add that he is an exciting artist to work with and lots of fun. I have a great deal of respect for him as an artist and a person."

Accounts from the other lithographers he works with are much the same. Peter Holmes has written an amusing little scenario titled *R. C. Gorman at Origins Press*, describing much the same activities in dramatic form. Aside from his instinctive need to extract fun out of every situation, there is a method to Gorman's madness: in order to produce the type of work he wants in the prodigious quantity he does, he needs to stay loose, and this is also true when he is sketching from a live model or painting.

Early in 1977 Gorman purchased land in Tubac, Arizona, and began plans for a house-gallery-studio complex there. It was a complete surprise to many people, but the idea had been germinating for several years. It began when he met Tubac resident Dr. Elizabeth Brownell at a cocktail party in Jackson Hole, Wyoming. She suggested and then arranged his first Tubac exhibit. This picturesque village about forty-five miles south of Tucson had attracted many artists over the past twenty years and combined some of the same ingredients which had drawn Gorman to Taos a decade earlier. Tubac's mixture of Indian-Mexican culture and its proximity to Mexico were appealing. The property Gorman bought was ideally located for his purposes — on the main village street of Tubac just east of the Tubac Art Center. He says the complex he is building will have "an Indian-Mexican flavor, a feeling similar to my Navajo Gallery in Taos. This will be Navajo Gallery, Tubac. I'll be commuting back and forth between the two."

Tubac had another plus factor: prior to Gorman's purchase of the land, Peter Holmes, whom he had known in Albuquerque when Holmes was working at Tamarind, had opened his lithography shop, Origins Press, in Tubac. This was in late October of 1976. In November Gorman began working on his first lithograph there. It was also the presence of potter Maxine Guy there which stimulated his interest in ceramics.

In November of 1977 Gorman had another one-man show at the Tubac Art Center. Shortly after, a feature on him appeared in the magazine section of one of the area's newspapers giving residents some wise advice: "Southern Arizona may think it achieved quite a coup when famed Navajo artist R. C. Gorman purchased a plot of land in Tubac and announced his intention to build a home, gallery, and studio there. But anyone planning to bask in the artist's reflected glory may not realize one small drawback — you have to catch him first."[35]

Early in 1978 Gorman had nine exhibitions scheduled for the year, and undoubtedly there will be more. In addition to this he conducted workshops in lithography at Yavapai Community College in Prescott, Arizona, and at Kansas State University. In May he was honored by Governor and Mrs. Jerry Apodaca with an exhibit in the rotunda of the New Mexico State Capital, Santa Fe. In September a Gorman retrospective was scheduled at Northern Arizona University, which he had attended in the 1950s. Sprinkled throughout his projected schedule, between the exhibition dates, are notations to "work at Western Graphics" or "work at Origins Press." His lithographs continue to be a very important part of his artistic production. Not scheduled yet, but one of Gorman's fondest hopes, is a father-and-son showing of lithographs. Carl Gorman reports: "R. C. has been encouraging me to do lithographs so we can have a show together. I did one lithograph way back at Otis Art Institute, but no others until now. So far I've completed three. They are based on the clan migration myths in the style of rock paintings and involving ancient Indian symbolism."

In January, 1978, Gorman took two weeks off to fly to Japan, "Just because I've always wanted to go there." He found it fascinating, and was especially impressed with its food. As friend Suzanne Brown said, "It's hard to get him off the subject. He's praised Japanese food so much, I'm developing a craving for it myself." In sharp contrast to his childhood when he often suffered hunger pangs, he has since been able to indulge his passion for food and has collected recipes from all parts of the world. These will be combined with another favorite subject, the nude figure, in his projected book, *Nudes and Food: Gorman Goes Gourmet.*

Of all the many projects and exhibitions scheduled for 1978, none was more important to Gorman than the event which took place in Ganado, Arizona, on May 27. On that day he received an honorary Doctorate of Fine Arts from The College of Ganado. The citation, presented to him by the president of the college, Thomas Carson Jackson, was read by Harris Richards, head librarian: "On the occasion of the sixth commencement of The College of Ganado we are proud to welcome back to this community an illustrious alumnus of Ganado Mission High School, the predecessor of The College. As a graduate in the Class of 1950 your ties to Ganado are strong. It was here at Ganado that Miss Jenny Louis Lind, an art teacher, fostered in a boy called Rudy the creativity and talent that became the artist the world knows today as R. C. Gorman. . . . You have brought many honors upon yourself and in so doing you have increased the awareness of the American people of the rich culture and tradition of the Navajo. The faculty and Board of Regents of The College of Ganado are honored to confer upon an individual whose name has become synonymous with 'modern American Indian art' the degree of Doctor of Fine Arts."

Among writers there is a saying when referring to the structure of a story: "The end is in the beginning," and this seems to be true of Gorman's life — the celebrated artist returning to receive honors, the small boy doing his first drawing in the sands of Canyon de Chelly. Despite the many new directions Gorman is taking, the new horizons still to be opened to him, there is a sense of his life coming full circle. Yet, according to the Navajo Way, a circle is never completed; rather, it is left open to allow a pathway to new achievements, a continuation and constant renewal of life.

1966-1970

GORMAN RECALLS the chance meeting which led him into the lithographic medium: "In 1966 I met Raul Anguiano at the Art Wagon Gallery in Scottsdale. He was one of the artists I admired when I was studying at Mexico City College, and I remember I was specially impressed with his famous lithograph of the woman pulling a thorn out of her foot. He encouraged me to try lithography and told me he would introduce me to his lithographer, José Sanchez in Mexico City. I don't remember the exact date, but I do remember I went to Mexico right away and that I did my first work in lithography that same year, 1966.

"At that time José Sanchez had his own lithography shop. In addition to Anguiano, he had done work for Siqueiros, Tamayo, and Orozco. I saw their lithographs on the walls of his studio. Sanchez had his whole family working for him —his kids were grinding stones and his wife was collating things. He had only one arm but he lifted those stones as if they were balls of cotton. It was strange for me, working with lithography for the first time, because Sanchez didn't speak English, just a few key words—so we grunted and made hand signals to each other. With that and my limited Spanish we managed to communicate."

Gorman recalls that the first lithograph he completed under Sanchez's tutelage was *Navajo Mother in Supplication*. It was featured on the cover of the *Indian Historian* in the Winter 1968 issue and in varying colors in three succeeding issues—Spring, Summer, and Fall 1969. The editors wrote: "This lithograph by R. C. Gorman has won first prizes and is becoming a classic in the art of Indian America." The Madonna or mother-and-child theme was a familiar one for him in his oil pastel drawings, thus it was a logical choice for a first effort in the new medium. There was some confusion in the dating of this edition—some are dated 1966 and some 1970. Gorman believes that he did not date the entire edition of 100 at the time of printing and that when he dated them later he confused the date with those done on a subsequent trip to Mexico. He recalls that on this second trip, the first one he did was *Three Navajo Women* and then *Three Taos Men*. He could not remember when he had finished *Woman Combing Hair* and *Woman with Blowing Hair*. These were discovered in early 1978 during an interview with Dr. Byron Butler. It is certain, however, that Gorman did them with Sanchez since they are printed on the same paper as his other Mexican lithographs and, like the others, do not have blindstamps or chops. The titles on these two are descriptive only, as no documentation has been found. Since they are done in a single color it would seem likely that Gorman did them before attempting the two-color works, *Three Navajo Women* and *Three Taos Men*.

THREE TAOS MEN   Dated 1970   Two Color   20 x 26 inches   José Sanchez

(WOMAN COMBING HAIR)   Dated 1970   One Color   26 x 20 inches   José Sanchez

THREE NAVAJO WOMEN   Dated 1970   Two Color   20 x 26 inches   José Sanchez

NAVAJO MOTHER IN SUPPLICATION   1966   One Color   20 x 26 inches   José Sanchez

(WOMAN WITH BLOWING HAIR)   Dated 1970   One Color   26 x 20 inches   José Sanchez

1971

GORMAN'S MEXICAN LITHOGRAPHS were shown at his gallery in Taos, but he had not yet become widely known in the medium when Dr. Byron Butler suggested forming a collaboration. As Dr. Butler tells it: "I had the idea of forming a partnership with R. C. to do suites of lithographs planned in advance as to subject and composition. Final details of the art and its execution were left to Gorman. I was to pay for the paper and printing. I also handled the packaging or portfolios for each suite, and the marketing."

By this time the Tamarind Institute had completed the move from its original Los Angeles location to a building adjacent to the campus of the University of New Mexico in Albuquerque and had begun its printing and training program in the fall of 1970. The Ford Foundation Grant which had helped to initiate and sustain its program during the 1960s was to be gradually withdrawn so that a large part of its printing would have to be privately financed by the artist or a sponsoring publisher. Butler went to Tamarind and had an interview with institute director Clinton Adams and Garo Antreasian. They agreed to have a meeting with Gorman, and as Gorman says, "Byron and I went to Albuquerque together and formed a joint venture and started the suites. I really enjoyed myself and he enjoyed it, too."

Their first collaborative effort was to be the suite *Homage to Navajo Women.* On October 11, 1971, Gorman drew a study of a woman on the stone with a lithographic crayon, and with a brush he applied a paste tusche diluted with water. It was titled *Contemplation,* and the printing of it was completed on October 22, 1971. On October 20, he did *Walking Women,* which was rendered in a completely different style; it was tighter and had more detail and contrast. *Contemplation,* on the other hand, was done in the loose rendering with a minimum of lines and detail which is more typical of his later work. When all of the lithographs were printed at the end of February, 1972, it was decided that *Contemplation* didn't fit into the general theme and feeling of the suite, so it was published as a single. In 1975 Gorman did another lithograph titled *Contemplation* in a similar style, but a smaller size.

One other lithograph begun in the fall of 1971, the lovely *Starry Night,* was also destined not to be included in *Homage to Navajo Women.* Gorman notes: "There was a technical problem in printing and we were only able to get an edition of twelve out of it." But two other lithographs begun in December, 1971, *Corn Mother* and *Young Navajo Woman,* were to be included in the suite.

CONTEMPLATION   October 1971   One Color   30 x 22 inches   Tamarind

1972

IN JANUARY AND FEBRUARY of 1972, Gorman completed the last two lithographs, *Noon Meditation* and *Mother and Child*, for the suite *Homage to Navajo Women*. The entire suite of five was printed in an edition of seventy by February 29. Dr. Butler had a cover and colophon page handprinted at the Plantin Press of Los Angeles on buff Arches paper to match the paper of the lithographs. The suite, along with *Starry Night* and several other individual lithographs, was presented at a preview party at the Executive House in Scottsdale on March 26. The lithographs were very well received, and the suite was purchased for a number of permanent collections including the Heard Museum of Phoenix, The Dallas Museum of Art, the Amon Carter Museum of Fort Worth, and the New Mexico Fine Arts Commission.

Having gained confidence from his first suite of lithographs, Gorman began another in May and completed it that same month. It consisted of six nude figures, three male and three female, and Gorman notes: "These were from an old sketchbook that I brought with me from San Francisco and had been done there from live models." Commenting on the fact that he was one of the first Indian artists to do the nude figure, Gorman observed: "I don't know what other Indians are afraid of as far as nudes go. It's very important to get down to the person's basic self. Isn't that what nude is?"[36] The title for the suite, *Bodies by Gorman*, was suggested by Gorman's friend Julian Garcia, an Albuquerque automobile dealer, who derived it from the famous old advertising slogan, "Bodies by Fisher." Again Dr. Butler's firm, Art Consultants, Ltd., was the publisher, and Butler had selected unique packaging for it—a lucite box which could be used either for shelf storage or as a frame for one of the lithographs.

In July Gorman began another nude study, *Man*, which proved to be one of his richest interpretations in the lithographic medium. It was printed in three runs from purple, brown, and red stones and executed with a lithographic crayon, rubbing crayon, and liquid tusche diluted with water and applied with a brush. It was selected for reproduction in the 1975 book *Art and Indian Individualists*, and appeared again in a review of the book in *Arizona Highways*, August, 1976.

This was followed in August by *Woman* or *Navajo Madonna*, a three-color lithograph in blue, brown, and pink. In September, Tamarind invited him to do a "guest edition." As Gorman explains: "Every now and then a workshop will give me a free stone to do anything I want at no charge." The result was *Taos Man*, a dramatic study of a hooded head, its masses of black on white paper giving the impression of a photographic negative, a concept Gorman was to develop further in his 1978 lithograph, *Reposing Woman*.

34

R.C. GORMAN

HOMAGE
TO
NAVAJO
WOMEN

1971-72

TAMARIND INSTITUTE

CORN MOTHER (Homage to Navajo Women Suite)   January 1972   One Color   30 x 22 inches   Tamarind

NOON MEDITATION (Homage to Navajo Women Suite)   February 1972   Two Color   22 x 30 inches   Tamarind

WALKING WOMEN (Homage to Navajo Women Suite) January 1972 One Color 30 x 22 inches Tamarind

MOTHER AND CHILD (Homage to Navajo Women Suite) February 1972 Two Color 30 x 22 inches Tamarind

YOUNG NAVAJO WOMAN (Homage to Navajo Women Suite)   January 1972   One Color   30 x 22 inches   Tamarind

TAOS MAN   September 1972   One Color   22½ x 18¼ inches   Tamarind

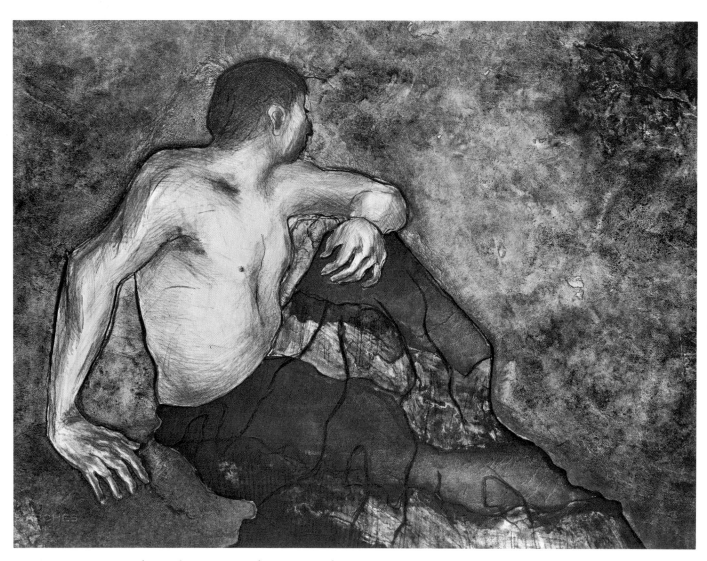

MAN   August 1972   Three Color   22 x 30 inches   Tamarind

R. C. GORMAN

BODIES
BY
GORMAN

JUNE 1972

TAMARIND INSTITUTE

FEMALE NUDE I (Bodies by Gorman Suite)   May 1972   One Color   15 x 12 inches   Tamarind

FEMALE NUDE II (Bodies by Gorman Suite)   May 1972   One Color   15 x 12 inches   Tamarind

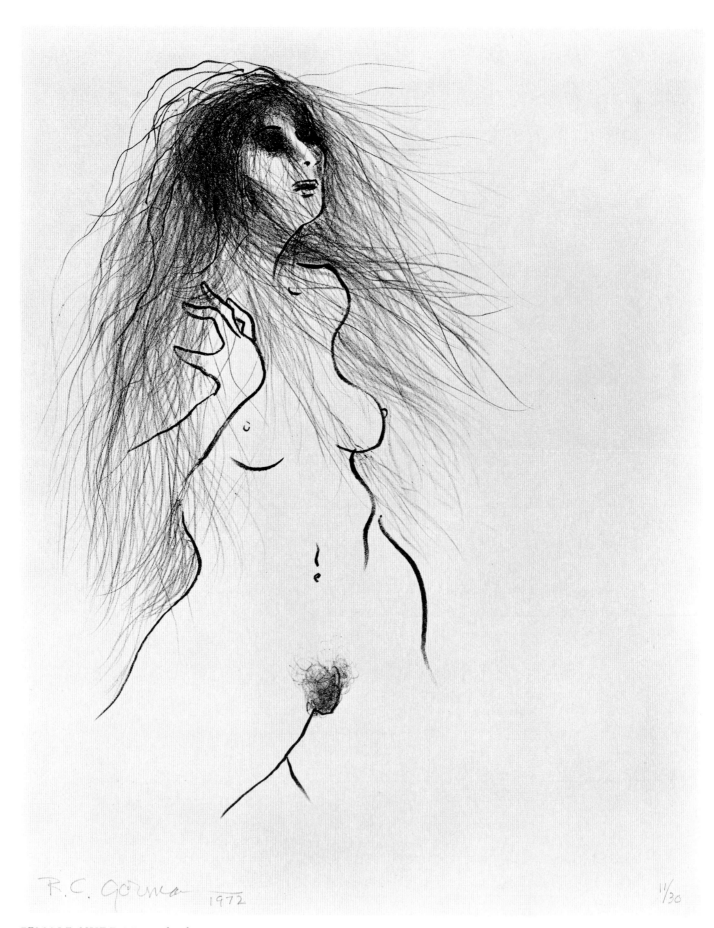

R.C. Gorman 1972   11/30

FEMALE NUDE III (Bodies by Gorman Suite)   May 1972   One Color   15 x 12 inches   Tamarind

MALE NUDE I (Bodies by Gorman Suite)   May 1972   One Color   15 x 12 inches   Tamarind

MALE NUDE II (Bodies by Gorman Suite)   May 1972   One Color   15 x 12 inches   Tamarind

MALE NUDE III (Bodies by Gorman Suite)   May 1972   One Color   15 x 12 inches   Tamarind

1973

FROM LATE NOVEMBER, 1972, through February of 1973, Gorman worked on a new suite at Tamarind which was to become one of his most memorable. He had lived in Taos almost five years and was feeling very much at home there. Appropriately, the suite was titled *Gorman in Taos*. It is a sensitive portrayal of the men and women of four New Mexico pueblos: Picuris, Taos, San Ildefonso, and Santo Domingo, all within easy reach of Taos and, consequently, familiar to him. *Picuris*, the first study, was printed in a single color, black. Dr. Butler notes that this drawing was a challenge for Gorman: "To distinguish the gender of figures bundled up in blankets is difficult, but Gorman, by concentrating detail on their faces, makes their male identity immediately apparent." In *San Ildefonso* the woman's clothes and the pottery are rendered with a minimum of lines, while the heavy concentration of color is reserved for the hair and upper background. It was printed in two runs, from a pink stone and a brown stone. *Taos*, a three-color lithograph, is perhaps the most dramatic and harks back to Gorman's early fascination with surrealism. The seven cloaked men, their thin, elongated figures huddled in a cluster against the background of the majestic Taos Mountains, seem to be responding to the age-old mystery of communion, as ancient as the mountain itself. The printing was done from a light brown zinc plate, a red, and a brown stone. Lithographic crayon was used to draw the images on the zinc plate and the red stone; applied with a brush on the brown stone were a paste tusche diluted in water and a mixture of triple-ink, lithotine and asphaltum. In *Santo Domingo*, Gorman achieves a surrealistic quality too, but of a more placid nature. The women selling the turquoise jewelry for which Santo Domingo is noted are a familiar sight; yet, here they seem to be isolated in time and space. It was printed in three runs from a tan stone, a turquoise zinc plate, and a brown stone. Dr. Butler had a portfolio specially designed for the suite—hard covers bound in silver and blue by Roswell Bookbinding of Phoenix, and lined with acid-free paper to protect the lithographs. This was a practice he followed for all the Gorman suites he published.

While the *Gorman in Taos* suite was in progress, Gorman was invited to do another guest edition at Tamarind and the result was *Self-Portrait*, the only self-portrait he has done in the lithographic medium. "I sketched it in the bathroom at Tamarind, looking in the mirror over the washbowl. I don't know why I added the glasses; I never wear them." The lithograph was printed in two states: a three-color run was printed first from a lavender, turquoise, and brown stone. The first two stones were then effaced and the brown stone held for a single-color run.

GORMAN
IN
TAOS

BY

R.C. GORMAN

1973

TAMARIND INSTITUTE

PICURIS (Gorman in Taos Suite)   December 1972   One Color   22 x 30 inches   Tamarind

SAN ILDEFONSO (Gorman in Taos Suite) December 1972 Two Color 30 x 22 inches Tamarind

SANTO DOMINGO (Gorman in Taos Suite) February 1973 Three Color 22 x 30 inches Tamarind

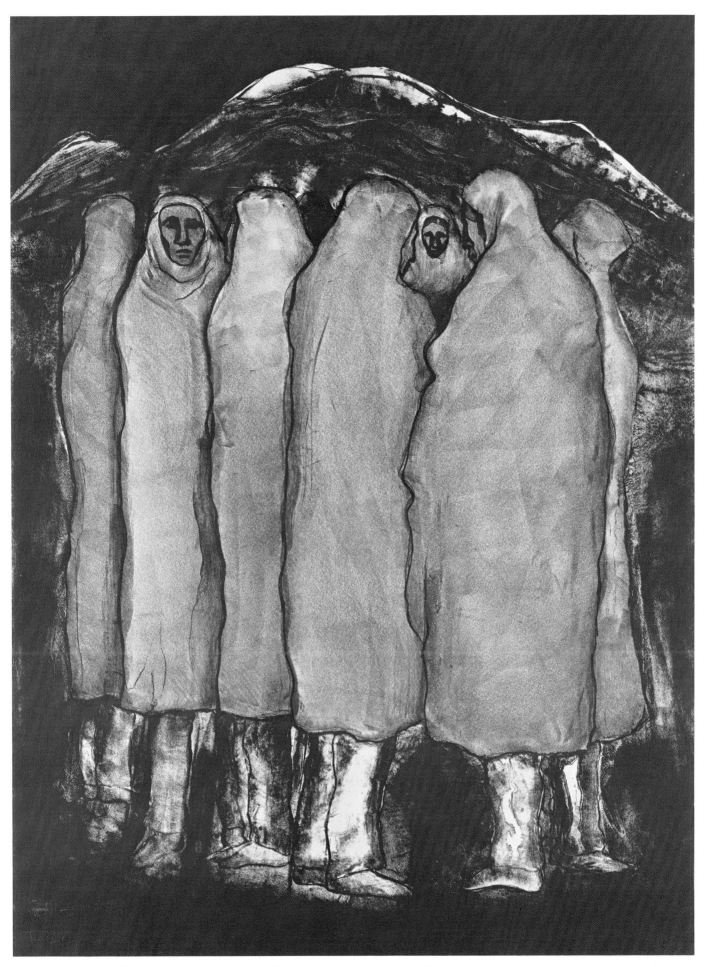

TAOS (Gorman in Taos Suite)   January 1973   Three Color   30 x 22 inches   Tamarind

A suite of original lithographs by

R. C. GORMAN

Drawn and hand printed at Tamarind Institute, Albuquerque, New Mexico, during the months of December 1972 through February 1973. The edition consists of sixty numbered impressions on buff Arches, measuring 22 by 30 inches, plus two Tamarind Impressions. In addition, several artist's and trial proofs exist and are recorded at Tamarind Institute.

The lithographs were printed by Ben Adams and Tamarind Master Printer Harry Westlund. All stones and plates have been effaced. Letterpress by the Plantin Press, Los Angeles. Portfolio by Roswell Bookbinding, Phoenix.

Published by Art Consultants, Ltd., Phoenix, Arizona.

A/p

R.C. Gorman 1973

SELF-PORTRAIT (Second State)　February 1973　One Color　13 x 9½ inches　Tamarind

1974

GORMAN'S FIRST COMPLETED WORK for 1974 was *Twilight Ladies* rendered in rich washes and printed in two states (as illustrated here). The term "states" refers to a printing variation of the same image. *Twilight Ladies* was first printed in an edition of twenty in a single color, sepia—the first state. The stone, rather than being effaced as is customary upon completion of printing, was held and inked with blue-purple, purple, and yellow in the blended inking method. Gorman then executed an image on a second stone, which was inked with dark brown. The images printed from the two stones resulted in a four-color lithograph, the second state, printed in an edition of forty. Upon completion of printing both stones were effaced. The record of printing for each state was documented, noting that the stone had been held from the first state for use in the second state. Gorman then began the *Nanabah* suite—studies of four women, also in two states, but here the multi-color version was printed first, with one of the stones held for printing the single-color second state. In both states Gorman hand-tinted the earrings in *Zonnie* and the bowl in *Tazbah* after printing. Three of the studies were reproduced in needlepoint by a Los Angeles firm—a first in this medium.

In May, Gorman began work on *Dez-bah*. He donated half of the edition of 140 to the Albuquerque Opera Guild to be sold by them as their major fundraising activity of the year in support of the Santa Fe Opera. By September 11, the printing of the suite *Homage to Spider Woman* was completed. According to Navajo legend, it was Spider Woman who taught the Navajos how to weave. Abstracted Navajo rug patterns were one of his most famous painting themes, but this was the first time he interpreted it in the lithographic medium. Dr. Butler notes: "This was the last suite we did together. Due to illness and other concerns, I was unable to continue, and the suite was not advertised much, but it received a great deal of admiration from museums and university art departments." In 1975 it was featured in Gorman's one-man exhibit at the Navajo Museum of Ceremonial Art (now the Wheelwright Museum) in Santa Fe.

Kneeling Woman was a guest edition at Tamarind, completed in July, and *Khisani*, another study of a woman, was done in November. "Khisani," Gorman notes, "is a Navajo word meaning 'they who have a house.' It was published by Ken Johns Lincoln Mercury of Albuquerque." In November he completed the last suite he was to do at Tamarind. *Reminiscences* included four lithographs, distinct in subject matter, rendering, and printing techniques. *Navajo Fire Dancer* and *Expectations* were printed simultaneously from the same stone on the same sheet of paper, and torn into separate editions after printing. *Mother and Child* and *Corn Lady* were done in the same way.

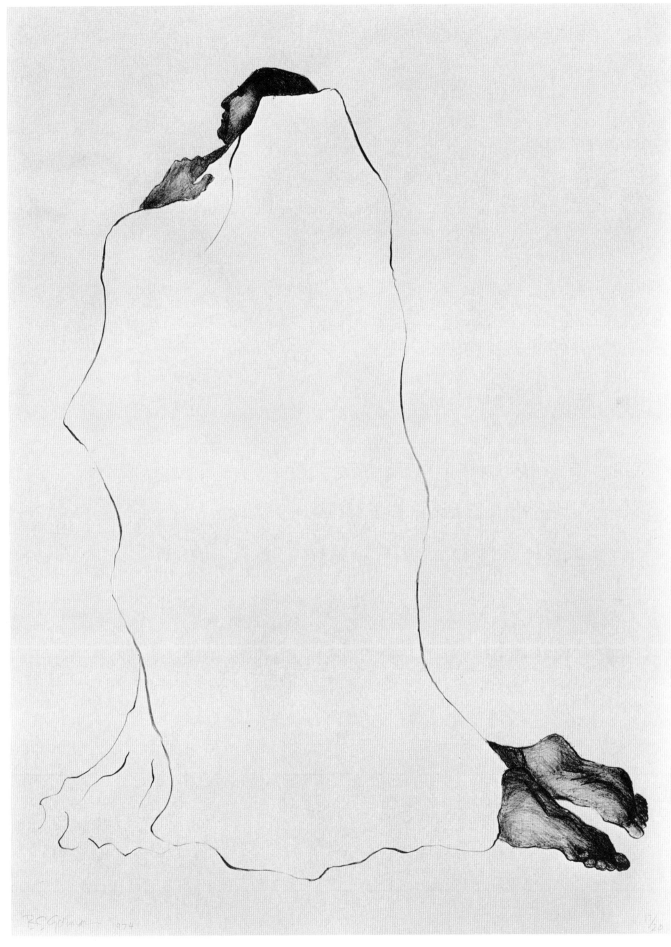

KNEELING WOMAN   September 1974   One Color   30 x 22 inches   Tamarind

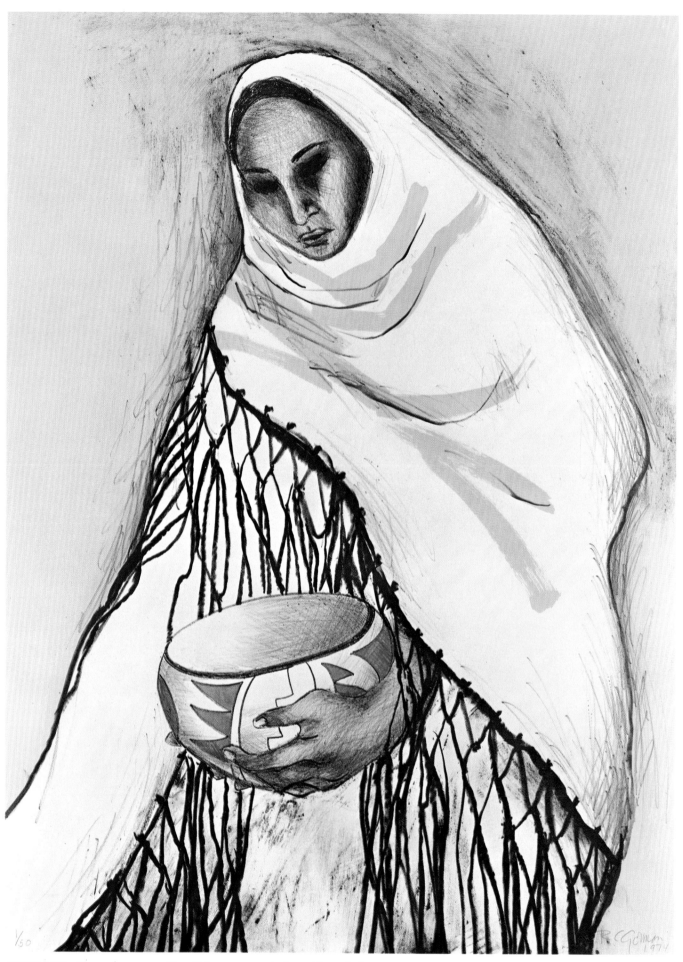

KHISANI   November 1974   Two Color   30 x 22 inches   Tamarind

DEZ-BAH   May 1974   Three Color   30 x 22 inches   Tamarind

TWILIGHT LADIES (First State)   January 1974   One Color   22 x 17 inches   Tamarind

TWILIGHT LADIES (Second State)　January 1974　Four Color　22 x 17 inches　Tamarind

ZONNIE (Nanabah Suite—First State)   January 1974   Two Color   30 x 22 inches   Tamarind

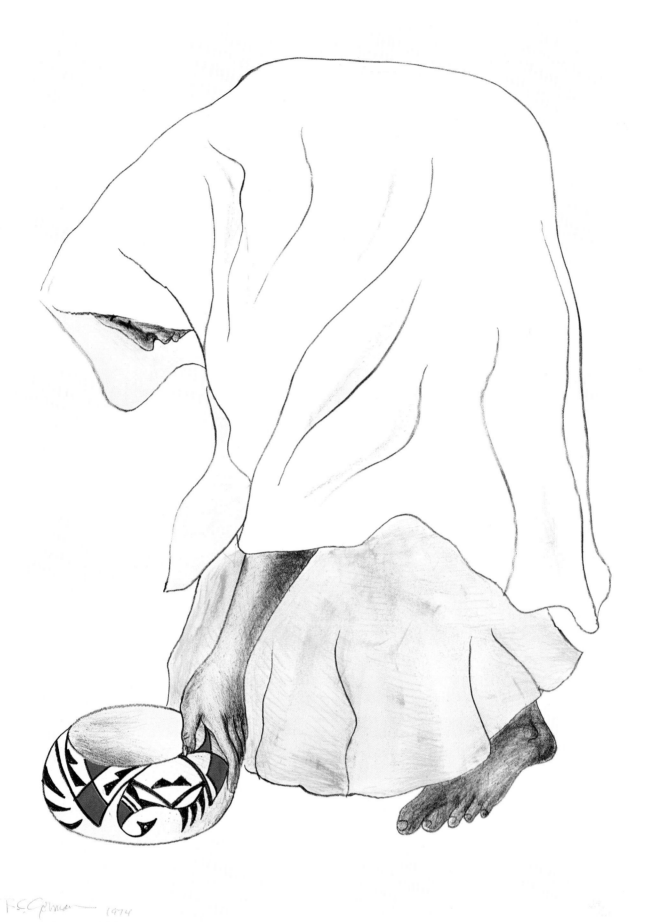

TAZBAH   (Nanabah Suite—First State)   March 1974   Three Color   30 x 22 inches   Tamarind

RUG NO. 1 (Homage to Spider Woman Suite) July 1974 Four Color 22 x 15 inches Tamarind

RUG NO. 2 (Homage to Spider Woman Suite)   August 1974   Five Color   22 x 15 inches   Tamarind

RUG NO. 3 (Homage to Spider Woman Suite)   July 1974   Six Color   22 x 15 inches   Tamarind

RUG NO. 4 (Homage to Spider Woman Suite)   September 1974   Two Color   22 x 15 inches   Tamarind

P.C Gorman 1974

A/P

CORN LADY (Reminiscences Suite)   November 1974   Four Color   15 x 11 inches   Tamarind

EXPECTATIONS (Reminiscences Suite)   November 1974   Six Color   15 x 11 inches   Tamarind

1975

YEI-BICHAI, a nine-color lithograph, was completed in late 1974 to be ready for the opening of Gorman's one-man exhibition at the Museum of the American Indian, New York, on January 29. The lithograph was published by the Heye Foundation in an edition of 150 and a poster was also made from it. Gorman had dealt with the Yei theme in his paintings, but this was the first time he interpreted it in the lithographic medium. He notes: "The lithograph was printed with three different color rolls." Often referred to as "rainbow rolls," or the "blended inking method," this procedure makes it possible to get a number of colors in a minimum of runs. In this case, several colors were applied to each of the three stones, thus achieving a nine-color lithograph in only three runs.

His next lithograph, *Homage to Seated Woman,* was also commissioned—by the Phoenix Art Museum League as part of their fund-raising activity. The scene at the Phoenix Art Museum party introducing the lithograph was featured in the KAET/Phoenix film on Gorman. He observes: "The party at the museum was planned to last for four hours, but they sold out in only two hours, so they had to end the party. Phoenix really supports its art!" Another work featured in the film was *Contemplation.* "I was shown doing this drawing from a live model in my studio. They had to do several retakes and I had to rework the face over and over again. For someone who likes to work quickly, as I do, that was certainly trying. Then Tamarind invited me to do it as a guest edition lithograph and we printed an edition of twenty." Tamarind had invited him to do another guest edition earlier in the year, and this resulted in *Mask No. 1–Monster Slayer No. 1.* When the Windmill Press opened in Taos, Gorman went there and completed three more masks. The four lithographs, as well as several acrylic paintings of masks were included in his one-man exhibition that fall at the Museum of Navajo Ceremonial Art (Wheelwright Museum) in Santa Fe. *Mask No. 2–Blue Kachina,* was featured on the cover of the exhibition catalog.

In August he returned to Tamarind to do *The Earring* which was commissioned by the Albuquerque Museum Association. It was the last lithograph he was to do at Tamarind Institute. Almost all of the printers he was to work with in the future were Tamarind graduates, and he had worked with many of them during his five-year association with the institute.

He did five more lithographs at Windmill Press during the year, including *Male Nude* and *Female Nude.* They were the first nudes he had done in the lithographic medium since 1972. "I haven't done any more nudes since these two. I'm sorry Windmill Press closed; since they were in Taos, I was able to go there and work whenever I wanted to."

CONTEMPLATION (II)   July 1975   One Color   15 x 22 inches   Tamarind

R.C. Gorman 1975

1/15

MASK NO. 2 (Blue Kachina)   May 1975   Three Color   16½ x 13½ inches   Windmill Press

MASK NO. 3 (Mudhead) July 1975 Six Color 16 x 13 inches Windmill Press

THREE WOMEN   October 1975   Two Color   13 x 16 inches   Windmill Press

THE EARRING   August 1975   Three Color   30 x 21¼ inches   Tamarind

MOTHER AND CHILD   July 1975   Four Color   20 x 23½ inches   Windmill Press

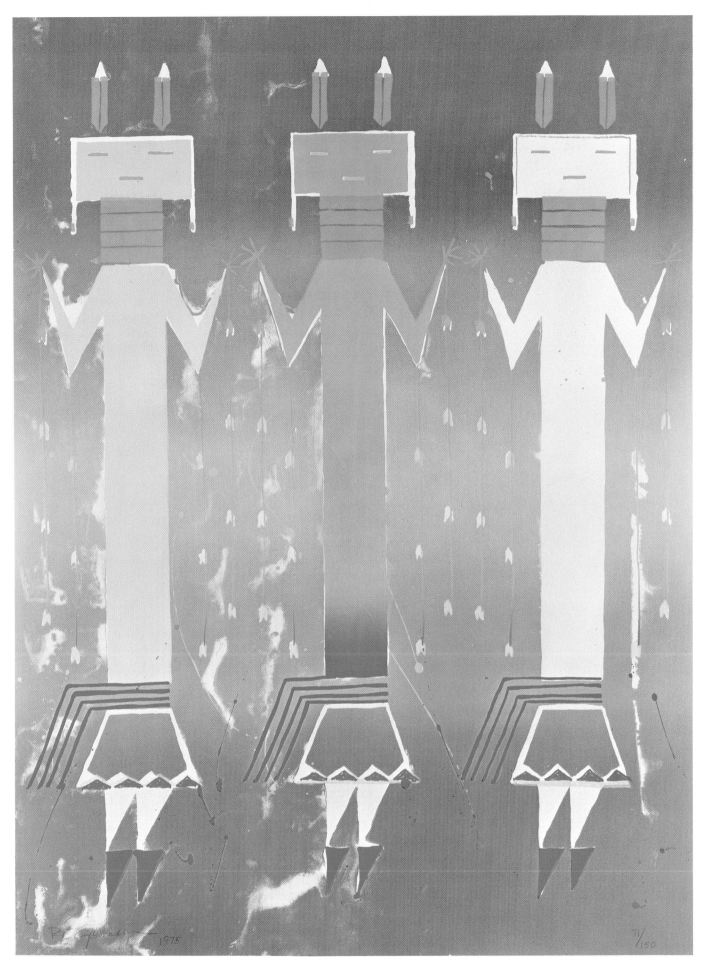

YEI-BICHAI December 1974 Nine Color 30 x 22 inches Tamarind

1976

THE GREAT VARIETY in Gorman's lithographic production for 1976 seems to indicate a transitional period, a search for new directions. Many of the works are a complete departure from any he had done during the six previous years. His first completed work in the year was the haunting and beautiful *Enigma* suite, the first suite he had done since 1974. Late in 1975, he began his first collaboration with Hand Graphics, Ltd., of Santa Fe and completed *Night*, the first study for the suite. It was followed by *Desert Man, Expectations,* and *Klah*, the latter two completed in January 1976. Of the last study, Gorman comments: "*Klah* is Hosteen Klah, the man who is responsible for what is now the Wheelwright Museum." When it was pointed out that the image bore some resemblance to Gorman, he agreed. "I had some photographs of Hosteen Klah to work from originally but the stone was ruined, so I had to do it over again and had to improvise. I call it 'my big sphinx in the desert.' When I finished it, I decided to go to Egypt, and I did the following year." In *Expectations* he points out: "Those are the Taos Mountains in the background." It is interesting to note that whenever Gorman depicts mountains, his work reflects a mystical quality and this is especially noticeable in this suite. Several different printing techniques were utilized. Only *Night* was printed solely from stones; the other three were printed from a combination of aluminum plates and stones with ink applied in the "rainbow roll" method which creates an effect particularly suitable to the surrealistic atmosphere of this suite. Later in the spring Gorman returned to Hand Graphics to complete two more studies for his mask series.

Another lithograph, started shortly after the *Enigma* suite, which also reflects his affinity for surrealism, is the lovely *Desert Women* (see frontispiece) where the three women seem to be walking in an endless and otherworldly desert. For this and two other studies of women, Gorman had traveled to Editions Press of San Francisco. Recently, Walter Maibaum, director of the press, noted: "R. C. says he feels a new freedom working in San Francisco; he feels more experimental and is stimulated by the city's international flavor."

In May, Gorman started working at still another lithography shop, Western Graphics of Albuquerque, and the second lithograph he executed there, the striking *Mountain Chant*, was also a drastic departure from anything he had done in the medium previously. Among the six studies of women he did at Western, several display new themes and approaches.

It was, perhaps, the constant change of environment, something Gorman has always thrived on, which contributed to the great variety achieved during this productive year.

MOUNTAIN CHANT   August 1976   Five Color   30 x 22 inches   Western Graphics

RECLINING LADY (Second State)   September 1976   Three Color   22 x 30 inches   Western Graphics

SPIDER WOMAN   December 1976   Four Color   30 x 22 inches   Western Graphics

WOMAN WITH BOWL June 1976 Four Color 22 x 30 inches Western Graphics

R. C. GORMAN

GORMAN / ENIGMA

1975-76

PYRAMID EDITIONS

NIGHT (Enigma Suite—Second State)   November 1975   Multi-color   22 x 30 inches   Hand Graphics, Ltd.

DESERT MAN (Enigma Suite)   November 1975   Multi-color   22 x 30 inches   Hand Graphics, Ltd.

EXPECTATION (Enigma Suite)   January 1976   Multi-color   22 x 30 inches   Hand Graphics, Ltd.

KLAH (Enigma Suite)   January 1976   Multi-color   22 x 30 inches   Hand Graphics, Ltd.

WAITING WOMEN   July 1976   Ten Color   22 x 30 inches   Editions Press

ARABESQUE   September 1976   Five Color   30 x 22 inches   Western Graphics

NAVAJO MOTHER   July 1976   Four Color   22 x 30 inches   Editions Press

WOMAN WITH CONCHO (Third State)   November 1976   Four Color   22 x 29 inches   Western Graphics

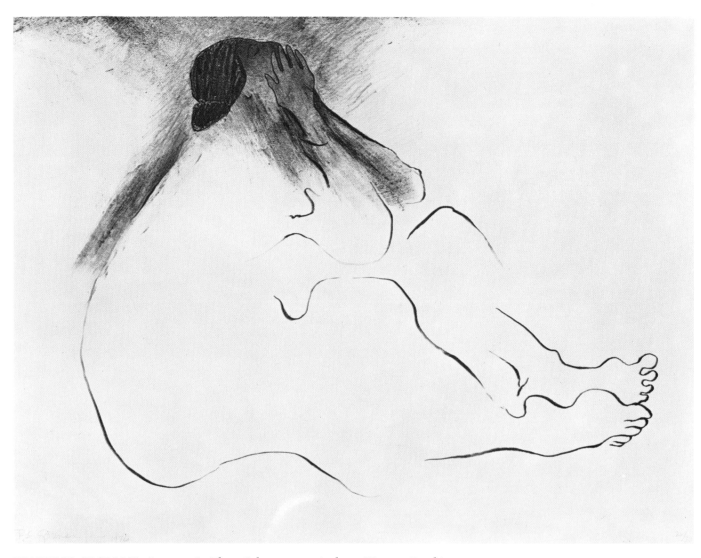

WAILING WOMAN   June 1976   Three Color   22 x 30 inches   Western Graphics

WOMAN WITH CHILI PEPPERS   June 1976   Five Color   30 x 22 inches   Western Graphics

1977

WHILE IN 1976 Gorman had been exploring new subject matter in his lithographs, in 1977 he returned to women exclusively. Keynoting this is his only suite of the year, titled simply *Women.* Among his sixteen 1977 studies, there were still some of his familiar "earth mother" types, but several others were taking on a new look: they were slimmer and had a certain chic and elegance about them. Typical of these and one of the loveliest is *Ya-na-bah,* his final lithograph for the year. In late November his cousin, Grace McCullah, came to visit him for a few days while he was staying in Tubac. One day she watched him work at Origins Press. His usual procedure is to sketch from a live model in his studio and then use the sketch as a guide while drawing on the lithographic stone. This time he had come unprepared. Grace recalls: "He sketched in the cloaked form of a seated woman but then exclaimed, 'I need a face!' He persuaded me to be his model. In all the years I have known him, which is all my life, this was the first time I had ever posed for him! I had watched him work before, but not in lithography. It was quite an experience. I was very pleased when he titled the lithograph *Ya-na-bah,* my Navajo name, and that it was selected for the dust jacket of his book." *Navajo Woman with Pears,* another "new look" executed in vibrant pastels, was featured on the cover of the Northland Press 1978 catalog. It was printed by Richard Newlin of Editions Press who also did *Desert Women,* frontispiece, the 1976 forerunner of his new approach.

Gorman has said: "Women are a constant challenge because their infinite variety invites an even greater infinity of interpretations." His works through the years have proven this to be true, and nowhere is it more vividly illustrated than among his first offerings for 1978. *Taos Pueblo Woman* shows some Mexican influence, but bears little resemblance to anything he has done before. The second state (not shown here) was done in eleven colors, with most of the additional color reserved for the shawl to which a floral pattern has been added, an innovative touch. *Indian Corn* is typical of his early and perennially popular oil pastel drawings in both technique and subject—the Navajo woman going about her chores. Of the sophisticated *Reposing Woman,* Gorman says: "It's completely different, a reversal; except for the face it's all black and where I've done my scrawling it's white. It's not a new technique, just something I haven't done before." Peter Holmes of Origins Press, where it was printed, has given an outline of the steps involved in printing this type of reversal print. There are ten steps, several of them repeated three to five times, illustrating the skill, infinite patience, and painstaking care involved in the production of quality lithographs, one of the reasons lithography has achieved a distinguished status in the art field.

NIGHT II (First State) January 1977 Five Color 22 x 30 inches Origins Press

WOMAN FROM PINE SPRINGS (First State)   November 1977   Six Color   30 x 22 inches   Western Graphics

NAVAJO WOMAN WITH PEARS   May 1977   Seven Color   22 x 30 inches   Editions Press

SINGING WOMAN   June 1977   Two Color   22 x 28½ inches   Western Graphics

POTTERY KEEPER (Women Suite—First State)   January 1977   Four Color   22 x 30 inches   Western Graphics

WOMAN FROM TUBAC   April 1977   Two Color   22 x 30 inches   Origins Press

WOMAN WITH MANTA (Women Suite)   July 1977   Four Color   30 x 22 inches   Western Graphics

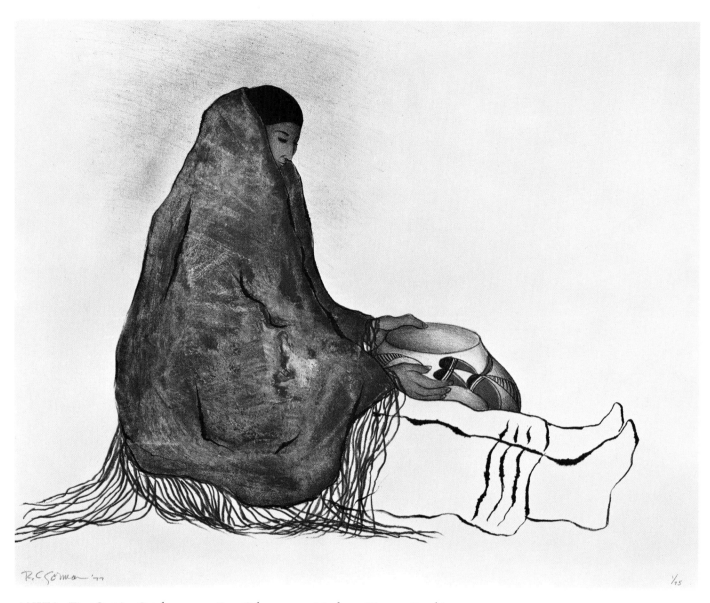

ANITA (First State)   October 1977   Four Color   21 x 26 inches   Western Graphics

WOMAN WITH PINK SHAWL (Women Suite)   September 1977   Four Color   22 x 30 inches   Western Graphics

WOMAN FROM INDIAN WELLS   October 1977   Six Color   22 x 30 inches   Origins Press

YA-NA-BAH   December 1977   Seven Color   30 x 22 inches   Origins Press

1978

DURING 1977 AND EARLY 1978 Gorman was commuting between Editions Press in San Francisco, Origins Press in Tubac, and Western Graphics in Albuquerque. Most of the printers with whom he was now working were known to him previously, an important factor, considering the compatible relationship which must exist between an artist and his printer. He had worked with Ben Q. Adams, for instance, since the early days at Tamarind, and when Adams established Western Graphics Workshop, he continued with him there. Adams notes: "We have a very good collaborative relationship. Since I have worked with him for six years, we understand each other well and I usually know what he needs in advance." He provides a brief outline of Gorman's working methods: "R. C. likes to arrive at the workshop early in the morning, around 8:00 or 8:30. The stones and all materials are laid out in advance of his arrival. Materials include Korn's lithographic pencils Nos. 2, 3, 4, and 5, La Favorite Tusche and solvents, Korn's slab crayons for broad work and razor blades for scraping, stick crayons for variety in line, and assorted brushes. Occasionally the drawing will involve washes or pounce work (a pounce is a tool made from a wooden spoon wrapped with cotton pads, nylon material, a chamois skin, and finally, with fine Japanese silk). The pounce surface is charged with rubbing ink and then pounded on the stone in the same way that an Indian would beat a drum. This leaves very soft tones over the surface that cannot be obtained in any other way. The washes R. C. uses are usually water, occasionally solvent, mixed with La Favorite Tusche and applied with a brush. One of his favorite techniques is to draw broad areas with slab crayon and pencils and then brush the crayon quickly with water to partially dissolve it, creating a combination wash and crayon look (see upper area of *Indian Corn*).

"Another technique R. C. often uses for background colors is to spray diluted Korn's liquid tusche through an air brush onto the stone or aluminum plate. This creates light, airy backgrounds and provides density and richness without the heavy look of a solid flat. Each lithograph produced by R. C. will involve most of these techniques in various combinations. He usually works on stone, with aluminum plates used for some under colors. He is particularly fond of our onyx marble stones. These create especially beautiful crayon work as the crystal patterns in the stones will show when the drawing is produced in a specific manner (see yellow dress on *Pottery Keeper*). He also likes the washes which can be created on onyx.

"Depending on the image, R. C. will work on a lithograph a very short time or several days. I have seen him draw an image (line drawing) in less than a half hour. However, lithographs of four or five colors will be drawn over a two- or three-day period."

INDIAN CORN   February 1978   Twelve Color   30 x 22 inches   Western Graphics

TAOS PUEBLO WOMAN (First State) January 1978 Six Color 26 x 20¼ inches Editions Press

REPOSING WOMAN   February 1978   Three Color   22 x 30 inches   Origins Press

Catalogue

THIS IS THE FIRST TIME an effort has been made to catalog the complete lithographic works of R. C. Gorman. The major portion of the information came from the print documentation provided by the six lithographers with whom Gorman has worked in the United States between 1971 and 1978. No formal documentation was found for the five works he completed in Mexico City between 1966 and 1970, and this is reflected here. Additional information was provided by the individual lithographers and some from Gorman's personal files.

In the print documentation the lithographer gives a complete and detailed record of the printing history of each lithograph. This includes materials used (stones, plates, inks, lithographic crayons and pencils, chemicals, brand and color of papers, etc.), the number of runs, methods used in preparing stones and plates, printing methods, as well as a list of impressions, beginning with the *bon`a tirer* (good to pull) which sets the standard against which all future prints are compared, trial proofs, color trial proofs, artist's proofs, sometimes printer's proofs, roman-numbered impressions or lithographer's impressions, one or two impressions to be retained as a record, and the artist's edition which is numbered in arabic and represents the major portion of the total printing. The number and type of each of the above may vary depending on the arrangement the artist has with the lithographer or publisher. Also included in the documentation is the "location of chops" on the printed lithograph. Each lithography shop, printer, and artist has his own chop (official stamp or seal) which is unique to him, and these are placed (usually embossed) in the lower left corner of the lithograph (the printer's chop sometimes appears in the lower right corner). What is important is the fact that all of these details are recorded, serving as a protection for the collector, the artist, and the lithographer. At the end of each print documentation is a statement dated and signed by the artist and printer, or printers: "All other proofs and impressions have been destroyed. The stones and plates have been effaced." It provides insurance that no other impressions exist or can exist in the future as "Original Prints" other than those described in the documentation.

Selected for this catalog are nine elements of the documentation considered to be of greatest interest to the general reader. The dates mark the month and year in which printing was completed; in the case of suites, several lithographs may have been printed earlier, but the completion of printing for the last lithograph in the suite determines the year under which the suite is listed. The paper size is noted in both inches and centimeters, and the height is given first. For the edition size, only the arabic-numbered artist's edition is noted. The publisher is listed last; no listing indicates the lithograph was published by the lithographer and/or Gorman.

An asterisk (*) indicates lithographs included in this book.

1966-1970

1. NAVAJO MOTHER IN SUPPLICATION*
1966, One Color
20 x 26 (50.8 x 66)
white paper (no watermark)
Edition of 100
Printed in Mexico City
by José Sanchez

2. (WOMAN COMBING HAIR)*
(Title not documented)
Dated 1970, One Color
26 x 20 (66 x 50.8)
white paper (no watermark)
Edition of 40
Printed in Mexico City
by José Sanchez

3. (WOMAN WITH BLOWING HAIR)*
(Title not documented)
Dated 1970, One Color
26 x 20 (66 x 50.8)
white paper (no watermark)
Edition of 25
Printed in Mexico City
by José Sanchez

4. THREE NAVAJO WOMEN*
Dated 1970, Two Color
20 x 26 (50.8 x 66)
white paper (no watermark)
Edition of 75
Printed in Mexico City
by José Sanchez

5. THREE TAOS MEN*
Dated 1970, Two Color
20 x 26 (50.8 x 66)
white paper (no watermark)
Edition of 100
Printed in Mexico City
by José Sanchez

1971

6. CONTEMPLATION*
October 1971, One Color
30 x 22 (76.2 x 55.9)
white Arches
Edition of 70
Tamarind Institute
Printed by John Butke

1972

7. WALKING WOMEN*
(Homage to Navajo Women suite)
January 1972, One Color
30 x 22 (76.2 x 55.9)

buff Arches
Edition of 70
Tamarind Institute
Printed by Wayne Simpkins
Art Consultants, Ltd.

8. YOUNG NAVAJO WOMAN*
(Homage to Navajo Women suite)
January 1972, One Color
30 x 22 (76.2 x 55.9)
buff Arches
Edition of 70
Tamarind Institute
Printed by Wayne Simpkins
Art Consultants, Ltd.

9. CORN MOTHER*
(Homage to Navajo Women suite)
January 1972, One Color
30 x 22 (76.2 x 55.9)
buff Arches
Edition of 70
Tamarind Institute
Printed by Wayne Simpkins
Art Consultants, Ltd.

10. NOON MEDITATION*
(Homage to Navajo Women suite)
February 1972, Two Color
22 x 30 (55.9 x 76.2)
buff Arches
Edition of 70
Tamarind Institute
Printed by Christopher Cordes
Art Consultants, Ltd.

11. MOTHER AND CHILD*
(Homage to Navajo Women suite)
February 1972, One Color
30 x 22 (76.2 x 55.9)
buff Arches
Edition of 70
Tamarind Institute
Printed by Harry Westlund
Art Consultants, Ltd.

12. STARRY NIGHT
February 1972, Two Color
22 x 30 (55.9 x 76.2)
buff Arches
Edition of 12
Tamarind Institute
Printed by Harry Westlund
Art Consultants, Ltd.

13. FEMALE NUDE I*
(Bodies by Gorman suite)
May 1972, One Color

15 x 12 (38.1 x 30.5)
buff Arches
Edition of 30
Tamarind Institute
Printed by Harry Westlund
Art Consultants, Ltd.

14. FEMALE NUDE II*
(Bodies by Gorman suite)
May 1972, One Color
15 x 12 (38.1 x 30.5)
buff Arches
Edition of 30
Tamarind Institute
Printed by Harry Westlund
Art Consultants, Ltd.

15. FEMALE NUDE III*
(Bodies by Gorman suite)
May 1972, One Color
15 x 12 (38.1 x 30.5)
buff Arches
Edition of 30
Tamarind Institute
Printed by Harry Westlund
Art Consultants, Ltd.

16. MALE NUDE I*
(Bodies by Gorman suite)
May 1972, One Color
15 x 12 (38.1 x 30.5)
buff Arches
Edition of 30
Tamarind Institute
Printed by Harry Westlund
Art Consultants, Ltd.

17. MALE NUDE II*
(Bodies by Gorman suite)
May 1972, One Color
15 x 12 (38.1 x 30.5)
buff Arches
Edition of 30
Tamarind Institute
Printed by Harry Westlund
Art Consultants, Ltd.

18. MALE NUDE III*
(Bodies by Gorman suite)
May 1972, One Color
15 x 12 (38.1 x 30.5)
buff Arches
Edition of 30
Tamarind Institute
Printed by Harry Westlund
Art Consultants, Ltd.

19. MAN (NAVAJO MAN)*
August 1972, Three Color

22 x 30 (55.9 x 76.2)
buff Arches
Edition of 70
Tamarind Institute
Printed by John Maggio
Art Consultants, Ltd.

20. WOMAN (NAVAJO MADONNA)
August 1972, Three Color
30 x 22 (76.2 x 55.9)
white Arches
Edition of 70
Tamarind Institute
Printed by Harry Westlund
Art Consultants, Ltd.

21. TAOS MAN*
September 1972, One Color
22½ x 18¼ (57.1 x 46.3)
Arjomari Arches
Edition of 20
Tamarind Institute, Guest Edition
Printed by Ben Q. Adams

1973

22. PICURIS (Gorman in Taos suite)*
December 1972, One Color
22 x 30 (55.9 x 76.2)
buff Arches
Edition of 60
Tamarind Institute
Printed by Harry Westlund
Art Consultants, Ltd.

23. SAN ILDEFONSO*
(Gorman in Taos suite)
December 1972, Two Color
30 x 22 (76.2 x 55.9)
buff Arches
Edition of 60
Tamarind Institute
Printed by Harry Westlund
Art Consultants, Ltd.

24. TAOS (Gorman in Taos suite)*
January 1973, Three Color
30 x 22 (76.2 x 55.9)
buff Arches
Edition of 60
Tamarind Institute
Printed by Ben Q. Adams
Art Consultants, Ltd.

25. SANTO DOMINGO*
(Gorman in Taos suite)
February 1973, Three Color
22 x 30 (55.9 x 76.2)
buff Arches
Edition of 60
Tamarind Institute
Printed by Harry Westlund
Art Consultants, Ltd.

26. SELF-PORTRAIT (First State)
March 1973, Three Color
15 x 12 (38.1 x 30.5)
buff Arches
Edition of 60

Tamarind Institute, Guest Edition
Printed by Ben Q. Adams
Art Consultants, Ltd.

27. SELF-PORTRAIT (Second State)*
February 1973, One Color
13 x 9½ (33.0 x 24.1)
buff Arches
Edition of 30
Tamarind Institute, Guest Edition
Printed by Ben Q. Adams
Art Consultants, Ltd.

1974

28. TWILIGHT LADIES (First State)*
January 1974, One Color
22 x 17 (55.9 x 43.2)
buff Arches
Edition of 20
Tamarind Institute
Printed by Ben Q. Adams
Art Consultants, Ltd.

29. TWILIGHT LADIES (Second State)*
January 1974, Four Colors
22 x 17 (55.9 x 43.2)
buff Arches
Edition of 40
Tamarind Institute
Printed by Ben Q. Adams
Art Consultants, Ltd.

30. NANABAH (Nanabah suite, First State)
January 1974, Two Color
22 x 30 (55.9 x 76.2)
white Arches
Edition of 70
Tamarind Institute
Printed by Ben Q. Adams
Art Consultants, Ltd.

31. ZONNIE (Nanabah suite, First State)*
January 1974, Two Color plus
Hand-Tinting by the Artist
30 x 22 (76.2 x 55.9)
buff Arches
Edition of 70
Tamarind Institute
Printed by Harry Westlund
Art Consultants, Ltd.

32. ANGELINA (Nanabah suite, First State)
February 1974, Two Color
30 x 22 (76.2 x 55.9)
white Arches
Edition of 70
Tamarind Institute
Printed by Ben Q. Adams
Art Consultants, Ltd.

33. TAZBAH (Nanabah suite, First State)*
March 1974, Three Color plus
Hand-Tinting by the Artist
30 x 22 (76.2 x 55.9)
buff Arches
Edition of 70
Tamarind Institute
Printed by Harry Westlund
Art Consultants, Ltd.

34. NANABAH
(Nanabah suite, Second State)
January 1974, One Color
22 x 30 (55.9 x 76.2)
buff Arches
Edition of 20
Tamarind Institute
Printed by Ben Q. Adams
Art Consultants, Ltd.

35. ZONNIE (Nanabah suite, Second State)
January 1974, One Color plus
Hand-Tinting by the Artist
30 x 22 (76.2 x 55.9)
white Arches
Edition of 20
Tamarind Institute
Printed by Harry Westlund
Art Consultants, Ltd.

36. ANGELINA
(Nanabah suite, Second State)
February 1974, One Color
30 x 22 (76.2 x 55.9)
white Arches
Edition of 20
Tamarind Institute
Printed by Ben Q. Adams
Art Consultants, Ltd.

37. TAZBAH (Nanabah suite, Second State)
March 1974, One Color plus
Hand-Tinting by the Artist
30 x 22 (76.2 x 55.9)
white Arches
Edition of 20
Tamarind Institute
Printed by Harry Westlund
Art Consultants, Ltd.

38. DEZ-BAH*
May 1974, Three Color
30 x 22 (76.2 x 55.9)
white Arches
Edition of 140
Tamarind Institute
Printed by Ben Q. Adams
Albuquerque Opera Guild

39. RUG NO. 1*
(Homage to Spider Woman suite)
July 1974, Four Color
22 x 15 (55.9 x 38.1)
white Arches
Edition of 70
Tamarind Institute
Printed by Lynn Baker
Art Consultants, Ltd.

40. RUG NO. 2*
(Homage to Spider Woman suite)
August 1974, Five Color
22 x 15 (55.9 x 38.1)
buff Arches
Edition of 70
Tamarind Institute
Printed by Lynn Baker
Art Consultants, Ltd.

41. RUG NO. 3*
(Homage to Spider Woman suite)
July 1974, Six Color
22 x 15 (55.9 x 38.1)
buff Arches
Edition of 70
Tamarind Institute
Printed by Lynn Baker
Art Consultants, Ltd.

42. RUG NO. 4*
(Homage to Spider Woman suite)
September 1974, Two Color
22 x 15 (55.9 x 38.1)
Copperplate Deluxe
Edition of 70
Tamarind Institute
Printed by Lynn Baker
Art Consultants, Ltd.

43. KNEELING WOMAN*
September 1974, One Color
30 x 22 (76.2 x 55.9)
Arjomari Arches
Edition of 20
Tamarind Institute, Guest Edition
Printed by James Reed

44. KHISANI*
November 1974, Two Color
30 x 22 (76.2 x 55.9)
Arjomari Arches
Edition of 50
Tamarind Institute
Printed by Lynn Baker
Ken Johns Lincoln Mercury

45. MOTHER AND CHILD
(Reminiscences suite)
November 1974, Four Color
15 x 11 (38.1 x 28)
white Arches
Edition of 70
Tamarind Institute
Printed by Ben Q. Adams
Western Art Gallery

46. CORN LADY (Reminiscences suite)*
November 1974, Four Color
15 x 11 (38.1 x 28)
white Arches
Edition of 70
Tamarind Institute
Printed by Ben Q. Adams
Western Art Gallery

47. EXPECTATIONS (Reminiscences suite)*
November 1974, Six Color
15 x 11 (38.1 x 28)
buff Arches
Edition of 70
Tamarind Institute
Printed by Stephen Britko
Western Art Gallery

48. NAVAJO FIRE DANCER
(Reminiscences suite)
November 1974, One Color plus
Hand-Tinting by the Artist

15 x 11 (38.1 x 28)
buff Arches
Edition of 70
Tamarind Institute
Printed by Stephen Britko
Western Art Gallery

1975

49. YEI-BICHAI*
December 1974 (signed 1975), Nine Color
30 x 22 (76.2 x 55.9)
buff Arches
Edition of 150
Tamarind Institute
Printed by Lynn Baker and Ben Q. Adams
Heye Foundation

50. HOMAGE TO SEATED WOMAN
February 1975, Six Color
22 x 30 (55.9 x 76.2)
buff Arches
Edition of 100
Tamarind Institute
Printed by Harry Westlund
Phoenix Art Museum League

51. MASK NO. 1
(Red Monster Slayer No. 1)
April 1975, Five Color
22 x 15 (55.9 x 38.1)
Arjomari Arches
Edition of 15
Tamarind Institute, Guest Edition
Printed by Harry Westlund
assisted by David Salgado

52. MASK NO. 2 (Blue Kachina)*
May 1975, Three Color
16½ x 13½ (41.9 x 34.3)
buff Arches
Edition of 15
Windmill Press
Printed by John Gruenwald

53. MASK NO. 3 (Mudhead)*
July 1975, Six Color
16 x 13 (40.6 x 33)
buff Arches
Edition of 50
Windmill Press
Printed by David Panosh

54. MASK NO. 4 (Apache)
October 1975, Five Color
16 x 13 (40.6 x 33)
buff Arches
Edition of 15
Windmill Press
Printed by John Gruenwald

55. CONTEMPLATION (II)*
July 1975, One Color
15 x 22 (38.1 x 55.9)
white Arches
Edition of 20
Tamarind Institute, Guest Edition
Printed by Ben Q. Adams

56. MOTHER AND CHILD*
July 1975, Four Color
20 x 23½ (50.8 x 59.7)
buff Arches
Edition of 50
Windmill Press
Printed by David Panosh
and John Gruenwald

57. THE EARRING*
August 1975, Three Color plus
Hand-Tinting by the Artist
30 x 21¼ (76.2 x 54)
Copperplate Deluxe
Edition of 50
Tamarind Institute
Printed by Lynn Baker
Albuquerque Museum Association

58. SLEEPING WOMAN
October 1975, Two Color
13 x 15½ (33 x 39.3)
buff Arches Cover
Edition of 35
Windmill Press
Printed by John Gruenwald

59. NIGHT (First State)
October 1975, Multi-color
22 x 30 (55.9 x 76.2)
buff Arches Cover
Edition of 30
Hand Graphics, Ltd.
Printed by Ron Adams
Pyramid Editions

60. MALE NUDE
October 1975, One Color
20½ x 17 (52.1 x 43.2)
buff Arches
Edition of 40
Windmill Press
Printed by John Gruenwald

61. FEMALE NUDE
October 1975, One Color
20½ x 17 (52.1 x 43.2)
buff Arches
Edition of 40
Windmill Press
Printed by John Gruenwald

62. THREE WOMEN *
October 1975, Two Color
13 x 16 (33 x 40.6)
buff Arches
Edition of 10
Windmill Press
Printed by John Gruenwald

1976

63. NIGHT (Second State, Enigma suite)*
November 1975, Multicolor
22 x 30 (55.9 x 76.2)
Rives BFK
Edition of 70
Hand Graphics, Ltd.

Printed by Ron Adams
Pyramid Editions

64. DESERT MAN (Enigma suite)*
November 1975, Multicolor
22 x 30 (55.9 x 76.2)
Rives BFK
Edition of 70
Hand Graphics, Ltd.
Printed by David Panosh
Pyramid Editions

65. EXPECTATION (Enigma suite)*
January 1976, Multicolor
22 x 30 (55.9 x 76.2)
Rives BFK
Edition of 70
Hand Graphics, Ltd.
Printed by Ron Adams
Pyramid Editions

66. KLAH (Enigma suite)*
January 1976, Multicolor
22 x 30 (55.9 x 76.2)
Rives BFK
Edition of 70
Hand Graphics, Ltd.
Printed by Ron Adams
Pyramid Editions

67. MASK NO. 5 (Navajo Born of Water)
February 1976, Multicolor
13½ x 16½ (34.3 x 41.9)
Rives BFK
Edition of 40
Hand Graphics, Ltd.
Printed by David Panosh

68. MASK NO. 6 (Red Mask No. 2)
May 1976, Multicolor
19 x 24⅝ (48.3 x 62.5)
Rives BFK
Edition of 30
Hand Graphics, Ltd.
Printed by David Panosh

69. WOMAN WITH CHILI PEPPERS*
June 1976, Five Color
30 x 22 (76.2 x 55.9)
buff Arches
Edition of 76
Western Graphics
Printed by Ben Q. Adams

70. WOMAN WITH BOWL*
June 1976, Four Color
22 x 30 (55.9 x 76.2)
buff Arches
Edition of 40
Western Graphics
Printed by Ben Q. Adams

71. WAILING WOMAN*
June 1976, Three Color
22 x 30 (55.9 x 76.2)
buff Arches
Edition of 30
Western Graphics
Printed by Richard Godbold

72. DESERT WOMEN
July 1976, Multicolor
22 x 30 (55.9 x 76.2)
white Arches
Edition of 120
Editions Press
Printed by Richard Newlin
Frontispiece

73. NAVAJO MOTHER*
July 1976, Four Color
22 x 30 (55.9 x 76.2)
buff Arches
Edition of 120
Editions Press
Printed by Richard Newlin

74. WAITING WOMEN*
July 1976, Ten Color
22 x 30 (55.9 x 76.2)
buff Arches
Edition of 120
Editions Press
Printed by Richard Newlin

75. MOUNTAIN CHANT*
August 1976, Five Color
30 x 22 (76.2 x 55.9)
buff Arches
Edition of 60
Western Graphics
Printed by Ben Q. Adams

76. ARABESQUE*
September 1976, Five Color
30 x 22 (76.2 x 55.9)
buff Arches
Edition of 75
Western Graphics
Printed by Ben Q. Adams

77. RECLINING LADY (First State)
September 1976, Two Color
22 x 30 (55.9 x 76.2)
white Arches
Edition of 20
Western Graphics
Printed by Richard Godbold

78. RECLINING LADY (Second State)*
September 1976, Three Color
22 x 30 (55.9 x 76.2)
buff Arches
Edition of 40
Western Graphics
Printed by Richard Godbold

79. WOMAN WITH CONCHO (First State)
September 1976, Two Color
22 x 29 (55.9 x 73.6)
white Arches
Edition of 50
Western Graphics
Printed by Richard Godbold

80. WOMAN WITH CONCHO
(Second State)
October 1976, Four Color

22 x 29 (55.9 x 73.6)
white Arches
Edition of 60
Western Graphics
Printed by Richard Godbold

81. WOMAN WITH CONCHO*
(Third State)
November 1976, Four Color
22 x 29 (55.9 x 73.6)
white Arches
Edition of 60
Western Graphics
Printed by Richard Godbold

82. SPIDER WOMAN*
December 1976, Four Color
30 x 22 (76.2 x 55.9)
white Arches
Edition of 100
Western Graphics
Printed by Richard Godbold
Dewey-Kofron Gallery

1977

83. NIGHT II (First State)*
January 1977, Five Color
22 x 30 (55.9 x 76.2)
white Arches
Edition of 70
Origins Press
Printed by Peter C. Holmes

84. NIGHT II (Second State)
January 1977, Two Color
22 x 30 (55.9 x 76.2)
white Arches
Edition of 30
Origins Press
Printed by Peter C. Holmes

85. NIGHT II (Third State)
January 1977, Four Color
22 x 30 (55.9 x 76.2)
white Arches
Edition of 40
Origins Press
Printed by Peter C. Holmes

86. NAVAJO WOMAN (First State)
January 1977, Four Color
14¾ x 12 (37.5 x 30.5)
Arjomari Arches
Edition of 75
Western Graphics
Printed by Ben Q. Adams

87. NAVAJO WOMAN (Second State)
January 1977, Five Color
14¾ x 12 (37.5 x 30.5)
German Etching
Edition of 30
Western Graphics
Printed by Ben Q. Adams

88. POTTERY KEEPER*
(Women suite, First State)

January 1977, Four Color
22 x 30 (55.9 x 76.2)
Arjomari Arches
Edition of 75
Western Graphics
Printed by Ben Q. Adams

89. POTTERY KEEPER (Second State)
January 1977, Two Color
22 x 30 (55.9 x 76.2)
white Arches
Edition of 30
Western Graphics
Printed by Ben Q. Adams

90. PEAR LADY
March 1977, Five Color
15 x 20 (38.1 x 50.8)
white Arches
Edition of 100
Western Graphics
Printed by Richard Godbold
Houston Art League

91. WOMAN FROM TUBAC*
April 1977, Two Color
22 x 30 (55.9 x 76.2)
buff Arches
Edition of 40
Origins Press
Printed by Peter C. Holmes
and Richard Frush

92. NAVAJO WOMAN WITH PEARS*
May 1977, Seven Color
22 x 30 (55.9 x 76.2)
white Arches
Edition of 90
Editions Press
Printed by Richard Newlin

93. KNEELING WOMAN (First State)
May 1977, Four Color
13 x 22 (33 x 55.9)
white Arches
Edition of 50
Western Graphics
Printed by Richard Godbold

94. KNEELING WOMAN (Second State)
May 1977, Two Color
13 x 22 (33 x 55.9)
buff Arches
Edition of 20
Western Graphics
Printed by Richard Godbold

95. SINGING WOMAN*
June 1977, Two Color
22 x 28.5 (55.9 x 72.5)
white Arches
Edition of 50
Western Graphics
Printed by Ben Q. Adams

96. WOMAN WITH MANTA*
(Women suite)
July 1977, Four Color

30 x 22 (76.2 x 55.9)
white Arches
Edition of 75
Western Graphics
Printed by Richard Godbold

97. MOTHER AND CHILD
(Women suite)
August 1977, Five Color
30 x 22 (76.2 x 55.9)
white Arches
Edition of 75
Western Graphics
Printed by Ben Q. Adams

98. WOMAN WITH PINK SHAWL*
(Women suite)
September 1977, Four Color
22 x 30 (55.9 x 76.2)
white Arches
Edition of 75
Western Graphics
Printed by Richard Godbold

99. LADY IN A YELLOW BLANKET
(First State)
October 1977, Six Color
20 x 16 (50.8 x 40.6)
buff Arches
Edition of 100
Western Graphics
Printed by Richard Godbold

100. LADY IN A BLANKET (Second State)
October 1977, Two Color
20 x 16 (50.8 x 40.6)
buff Arches
Edition of 50
Western Graphics
Printed by Richard Godbold

101. ANITA (First State)*
October 1977, Four Color
21 x 26 (53.3 x 66)
buff Arches
Edition of 75
Western Graphics
Printed by Ben Q. Adams

102. ANITA (Second State)
October 1977, Two Color
21 x 26 (53.3 x 66)
buff Arches
Edition of 50
Western Graphics
Printed by Ben Q. Adams

103. WOMAN FROM INDIAN WELLS*
October 1977, Six Color
22 x 30 (55.9 x 76.2) white Arches
Edition of 70
Origins Press
Printed by Peter C. Holmes
and Richard Frush

104. WOMAN FROM PINE SPRINGS*
(First State)
November 1977, Six Color

30 x 22 (76.2 x 55.9) white Arches
Edition of 75
Western Graphics
Printed by Ben Q. Adams

105. WOMAN FROM PINE SPRINGS
(Second State)
December 1977, Three Color
30 x 22 (76.2 x 55.9) buff Arches
Edition of 40
Western Graphics
Printed by Ben Q. Adams

106. YA-NA-BAH*
December 1977, Seven Color
30 x 22 (76.2 x 55.9)
white Arches
Edition of 100
Origins Press
Printed by Peter C. Holmes
and Richard Frush
Mary Martin and R. C. Gorman

1978

107. TAOS PUEBLO WOMAN (First State)*
January 1978, Six Color
26 x 20¼ (66 x 51.4)
buff Arches
Edition of 50
Editions Press
Printed by Donald Farnsworth
and Evelyn Lincoln

108. TAOS PUEBLO WOMAN
(Second State)
January 1978, Eleven Color
26 x 20¼ (66 x 51.4)
buff Arches
Edition of 50
Editions Press
Printed by Evelyn Lincoln

109. INDIAN CORN*
February 1978, Twelve Color
30 x 22 (76.2 x 55.9)
Arjomari Arches
Edition of 150
Western Graphics
Printed by Ben Q. Adams and Chris Fox

110. REPOSING WOMAN*
February 1978, Three Color
22 x 30 (55.9 x 76.2)
Rives BFK
Edition of 60
Origins Press
Printed by Peter C. Holmes
and Richard Frush

General Reference Works

Adair, John. *The Navajo and Pueblo Silversmiths.* Norman: University of Oklahoma Press, 1946.

Amplified Bible. Grand Rapids, Mich.: Zondervan Corp., 1976.

Antreasian, Garo Z., with Adams, Clinton. *The Tamarind Book of Lithography: Art and Techniques.* Tamarind Lithography Workshop, Inc., Los Angeles. New York: Harry N. Abrams, Inc., Publishers, 1971.

Brown, Dee. *Bury My Heart at Wounded Knee.* New York: Holt, Rinehart & Winston, 1970.

Canaday, John. *Mainstreams of Modern Art.* New York: Simon & Schuster, 1959.

Caso, Alfonso; Toussaint, Manuel; Montenegro, Roberto; Covarrubias, Miguel. *Twenty Centuries of Mexican Art.* Introduction by Antonio Castro Leal. The Museum of Modern Art, New York, in collaboration with the Mexican Government. Mexico City: Cia. Litográfica "La Enseñanza Objetiva," S.A., 1940.

Chaet, Bernard. *The Art of Drawing.* New York: Holt, Rinehart and Winston, 1978.

Chumacero, Alí. *Zuñiga.* With autobiographical notes by Francisco Zuñiga. Mexico City: Galeria de Arte Misrachi, 1969.

Franciscan Fathers. *Ethnologic Dictionary of the Navajo Language,* Saint Michaels, Arizona, 1910.

Gorman, Carl. "Carl Gorman Says Power to Heal Is Not Superstition." *Navajo Times,* 7 March 1974.

Heller, Jules. *Printmaking Today.* 2d ed. rev. New York: Holt, Rinehart and Winston, 1972.

Hopkins, Jon H. *Orozco: A Catalogue of His Graphic Works.* Flagstaff: Northern Arizona University Publications, 1967.

Man, Felix H. *Artists' Lithographs: A World History from Senefelder to the Present Day.* New York: G. P. Putnam's Sons, 1970.

McLain, Jerry. "Dr. Big: A Visit to Ganado's Presbyterian Mission." *Arizona Highways,* August 1948.

Navajo Times. "Slender Maker of Silver." 10 September 1970.

————. "Carl Gorman Retires . . . But Not for Long." 30 September 1976.

Neuvillate, Alfonso de. *Pintura Actual Mexico 1966* (Actual Painting: Mexico 1966). Mexico City: Artes De Mexico y Del Mundo, S.A., 1966.

Ross, John, and Romano, Clare. *The Complete Screenprint and Lithograph.* New York: The Free Press, a division of Macmillan Publishing Co., Inc., 1974.

Salsbury, Clarence G., M.D., with Hughes, Paul. *The Salsbury Story: A Medical Missionary's Lifetime of Public Service.* Tucson: University of Arizona Press, 1969.

Woodward, Arthur. *Navajo Silver: A Brief History of Navajo Silversmithing.* 1938. New edition. Flagstaff: Northland Press, 1971.

Notes

1. *Indian Historian* 1968, p. 23
2. Wood 1974
3. Ewing 1971, p. 4
4. *Psalms* 65:8
5. Brown 1970, pp. 23–36
6. Adair 1946, p. 22
7. Ibid.
8. *Navajo Times* 1970
9. *Franciscan Fathers* 1910, p. 430
10. KAET/Phoenix Film 1976
11. Salsbury 1969, p. 112
12. Ibid., p. 108

13. McLain 1948, pp. 4–11
14. Salsbury 1969, pp. 15–17
15. Buddecke 1972, p. 55
16. Chumacero 1969, p. 34
17. Scottsdale National Indian Arts Council 1970, p. 1
18. Manchester tape 1973
19. Snodgrass 1965, p. 30
20. Dunn 1972, p. 162
21. Carl Gorman 1974
22. Salsbury 1969, p. 111
23. Tanner 1973, p. 373
24. Canaday 1959, p. 440

25. Ewing 1971, p. 6
26. Antreasian and Adams 1971, p. 14
27. Tanner 1973, p. 371
28. Bucklew 1971
29. Ibid.
30. Wood 1974
31. Glauber 1976
32. Dockstader 1975
33. Ibid., Letter to Museum Members
34. Chumacero 1969, p. 31
35. Sowell 1977, p. 9
36. KAET/Phoenix Film 1976

Selected Bibliography

BOOKS

Bahti, Tom. *Southwestern Indian Arts and Crafts*. Flagstaff: K. C. Publications, 1966.

Brody, J. J. *Indian Painters and White Patrons*. Albuquerque: University of New Mexico Press, 1971.

Counter, Constance, and Tani, Karl. *Palette in the Kitchen*. Santa Fe: Sunstone Press, 1974.

Dictionary of International Biography. London, 1968–1971.

Findley, Rowa. *Great American Deserts*. Washington, D.C.: National Geographic Society, 1972.

Gridley, Marion E., ed. and comp. *Indians of Today*. 4th ed. rev. Chicago: I.C.F.P., Inc., 1971.

Highwater, Jamake. *Song from the Earth: American Indian Painting*. Boston: New York Graphic Society, 1976.

Klein, Bernard, and Icolari, Daniel, eds. *Encyclopedia of the American Indian*. New York: K. B. Klein & Co., 1967.

Masterworks from the Museum of the American Indian. New York: The Metropolitan Museum of Art, 1973. Front and back covers feature Gorman art.

Milton, John R., ed. *The American Indian Speaks*. Vermillion, S.D.: Dakota Press, University of South Dakota, 1969.

Monthan, Guy and Doris. *Art and Indian Individualists: The Art of Seventeen*

Contemporary Southwestern Artists and Craftsmen. Flagstaff: Northland Press, 1975.

Morrill, Claire. *A Taos Mosaic.* Albuquerque: University of New Mexico Press, 1973.

100 Years of Native American Painting. Oklahoma City: Oklahoma Museum of Art, 1978.

Rosen, Kennneth, ed. *The Man to Send Rain Clouds: Contemporary Stories by American Indians.* New York: Viking Press, 1974. Illustrated by R. C. Gorman and Aaron Yava. Short story by Gorman.

Snodgrass, Jeanne O. *American Indian Painters: A Biographical Directory.* New York: Museum of the American Indian, Heye Foundation, 1968.

Tanner, Clara Lee. *Southwest Indian Painting: A Changing Art.* 2d ed. rev. Tucson: University of Arizona Press, 1973.

Who's Who in America. Chicago: Marquis Who's Who, Inc., 1976–1977.

Who's Who in American Art. New York and London: Jaques Cattell Press. R. R. Bowker Co., 1973, 1976.

Who's Who in the West. Chicago: Marquis Who's Who, Inc., 1976–1977.

JOURNALS AND MAGAZINES

Aufmwasser, Achim, with photographs by Klaus Appel. "Bilder Vom Roten Mann: R. C. Gorman." *Mode Und Wohnen,* Issue 2, 1978.

Buddecke, Martha. "R. C. Gorman: Fun Loving Artist." *Southwest Art Gallery Magazine,* September 1972.

Business Week. "Investing in Young Artists," May 3, 1976.

DeLauer, Marjel. "American Indian Artist: R. C. Gorman." *Arizona Highways,* August 1976.

Dockstader, Frederick J. "R. C. Gorman: January 29–March 29, 1975." *Museum of the American Indian Exhibit Leaflet No. 9,* January 1975.

Dunn, Dorothy. "A Documented Chronology of Modern American Indian Painting in the Southwest." *Plateau.* Flagstaff: Museum of Northern Arizona, Spring 1972.

Ewing, Robert A. "An Indian and His Art: This Is Gorman." *New Mexico Magazine,* Spring 1971.

Gibson, Ellery. "Do You Suffer With TT's?" *School Arts Magazine,* June 1956. Four cartoons by R. C. Gorman illustrating article.

Grover, J. Z. "A Brief Introduction to Southwest Indian Art." *Arizona Highways,* August 1976.

Indian Historian. "Gorman Father and Son Exhibit Slated for San Francisco." May 1967.

————. "Museum of Indian Arts to Present R. C. Gorman." Winter 1968, p. 23. R. C. Gorman lithograph, "Navajo Mother in Supplication," on cover of this issue and three succeeding issues: Spring 1969, Summer 1969, Fall 1969.

LaRiviere, Anne L. "New Art by the Oldest Americans." *Westways Magazine,* May 1973.

Leal, Ronald. "R. C. Gorman: The Two Worlds of a Navajo Artist." *Mankind: The Magazine of Popular History,* vol. 2, no. 9, 1970.

Marcus, Hal. "R. C. Gorman: Indian Giver." *The Southwestern Art Form,* October 1977.

Meek, James. "Taos Today." *Southwest Art,* December 1973.

Molina, Olga. "Navajo Artist Captures Fleeting Beauty." *The News World.* 3 January 1978.

Monthan, Guy and Doris. "The Unpredictable R. C. Gorman." *American Indian Art Magazine,* Summer 1978.

Nelson, Mary Carroll. "R. C. Gorman: Navajo in Vogue." *American Artist,* September 1974.

New, Lloyd Kiva. "The Crafts of the Indian: A New Vitality Rekindles Proud Fires of the Past." *House Beautiful,* June 1971.

Oxendine, Lloyd E. "23 Contemporary Indian Artists." *Art in America,* July-August 1972.

Palm Springs Life. "R. C. Gorman: Neo-primitive Paintings Embrace Two Worlds as One." October 1969.

Reed, Michael. "Art Prints of the Southwest." *Southwestern Art Journal,* Winter 1976–1977.

Santa Fean Magazine. "R. C. Gorman, Artist." August 1976. Cover feature.

Schmitz, Tony. "Film Makers' Reflections . . . on the production of the American Indian Artists series." *Arizona Highways,* August 1976.

Snodgrass, Jeanne O. "Indian Art Today." *Western Review,* Winter 1965.

Southwest Art. "Nanabah." May 1974. Nanabah lithograph featured.

Sowell, Carol. "R. C. Gorman: A major Indian artist comes to Tubac." *Easy Living Magazine,* December 1977. Cover feature.

Wilks, Flo. "Gorman's Art Speaks of His Native Southwest to People Worldwide." *New Mexico Stockman,* September 1977.

NEWSPAPERS

Arizona Living. "Artist Reception at the Byron Butlers." 18 June 1971.

———. "A Phoenix First: R. C. Gorman's 'Homage to Navajo Women.' " 24 March 1972.

Austin Citizen, Marquee. "Navajo Artist to Show Lithographs Sept. 17." 9 September 1977.

Bryan, Howard. "The Creative Minds of Taos: 'Picasso of Indian Painters.' " *Albuquerque Tribune,* 1 May 1975.

Bucklew, Joan. "Art." *Arizona Republic,* 14 March 1971.

Foreman, T. E. "A Contemporary Painter, Who Happens to be Indian, Rejects Labeling His Work." *Riverside Daily Enterprise,* 19 May 1971.

Fosberg, S. Joslyn. "Populism: New Trend in Art." *New Orleans Vieux Carre Courier,* 22 January 1976.

Glauber, Robert. "The Superlative Indian Artist: R. C. Gorman." *Chicago Skyline,* 26 May 1976.

Jordan, George E. "Print Showing Should Appeal." *New Orleans Times-Picayune,* 11 January 1976.

Los Angeles Herald-Examiner, California Living. "Art." 30 May 1971.

McDaniel, C. G. "Navajo Artist Keyhole View." *San Jose Mercury News,* 6 June 1976.

Navajo Times. "R. C. Gorman's Paintings Relate Navajo Heritage." 2 September 1971.

———. "Ganado College Confers Degrees." 20 April 1978.

Perlman, Barbara. "R. C. Gorman: The Artist Who Laughs." *Scottsdale Daily Progress,* 10 February 1978.

Spengler, David. "Art from Artistry: Indian Spans Tradition, Avant-garde." *Bergen County Record* (New Jersey), 30 January 1975.

Tucson Daily Citizen. "Tubac Has Gorman Art." 4 December 1971.

Wilks, Flo. "R. C. Gorman's Paintings Relate Heritage to Navajo Women in Contemporary Society." *Albuquerque Journal,* 15 August 1971.

———. "Navajo Artist R. C. Gorman Completes Lithograph Suite." *Albuquerque Journal,* 3 February 1974.

Wilson, Maggie. "Gorman, Scholder—World's Leading Painters of Indians." *Arizona Republic,* 23 November 1975.

Wood, Harry. "Gorman Paintings Embody Rotund Figures." *Scottsdale Daily Progress,* 22 November 1974.

FILMS

R. C. Gorman. Thirty-minute film produced by KAET Television, Phoenix, Arizona, aired nationally over Public Broadcasting Service stations, August, 1976.

NBC's *Today Show.* Segment on R. C. Gorman aired nationally, June 13, 1978.

PUBLIC COLLECTIONS

El Paso Museum of Art, El Paso, Texas

Gonzaga University, Pacific Northwest Indian Center, Spokane, Washington

Heard Museum, Phoenix, Arizona

Indian Arts and Crafts Board Collection, U. S. Department of the Interior, Washington, D.C.

Indianapolis Museum of Art, Indianapolis, Indiana

Metropolitan Museum of Art, New York, New York

Museum of the American Indian, Heye Foundation, New York, New York

Museum of Indian Arts, American Indian Historical Society, San Francisco, California

Museum of Northern Arizona, Flagstaff, Arizona

Navajo Tribal Museum, Window Rock, Arizona

New Mexico Museum of Fine Arts, Santa Fe, New Mexico

Philbrook Art Center, Tulsa, Oklahoma

U. S. Department of the Interior, Bureau of Indian Affairs, Washington, D.C.

ONE-MAN EXHIBITIONS *(Selected)*

Coffee Gallery, San Francisco, California (1963)

Museum of Indian Arts, San Francisco, California (1966)

Student Union of the University of California, Berkeley (1966)

Manchester Gallery, Taos, New Mexico (1965, 1966, 1968)

Heard Museum, Phoenix, Arizona (1967)

Navajo Community College, Many Farms, Arizona (May 1970)

Northern Arizona University Art Gallery, Flagstaff, Arizona (1970)

Gallery of Modern Art, Scottsdale, Arizona (1971)

Jamison Gallery, Santa Fe, New Mexico (September 1973)

Aspen Gallery of Art, Aspen, Colorado (June 1973, February 1974, August 1974)

Baylor University, Waco, Texas (March 1974)

Wartburg College, Waverly, Iowa (November 1974)

Museum of the American Indian, Heye Foundation, New York, New York (1975)

Museum of Navajo Ceremonial Art (Wheelwright Museum), Santa Fe, New Mexico (1975)

van Straaten Gallery, Chicago, Illinois (1976)

Gallery of New Mexico, Santa Fe, New Mexico (1976)

Freeman-Anacker Gallery, New Orleans, Louisiana (1976)

Stables Gallery, Taos, New Mexico (1973, 1975, 1977)

White Buffalo Gallery, Wichita, Kansas (1976, 1977)

Walton Gallery, San Francisco, California (1977)

Clarke-Benton Gallery, Santa Fe, New Mexico (1977)

Santa Fe East, Austin, Texas (1977)

Marjorie Kaufman Gallery, Houston, Texas (1977)

Tubac Center of the Arts, Tubac, Arizona (1977)

Clay Gallery, New York, New York (1977)

Tigua Indian Reservation, El Paso, Texas (1977)

Muirhead Gallery, Costa Mesa, California (1978)

Suzanne Brown Art Wagon Gallery, Scottsdale, Arizona (1973, 1974, 1978)

Governor's Gallery, Rotunda of State Capitol, Santa Fe, New Mexico (1978)

AWARDS AND HONORS *(Selected)*

All American Indian Days Arts Exhibition, Sheridan, Wyoming, First Award

American Indian Artists, First Annual Exhibition, Kaiser Center, Oakland, California, Grand Award

Center of Arts for Indian America, Washington, D.C., Honorable Mention

Heard Museum Indian Arts and Crafts Show, Phoenix, Arizona, First Award and Honorable Mention

Honor Guard, City of San Antonio, Texas

Honorary Doctorate of Fine Arts, The College of Ganado, Ganado, Arizona

Included in Year-Long Exhibition at Vice-Presidential Mansion, Washington, D.C.

Key to the City of El Paso, Texas

National Cowboy Hall of Fame, Oklahoma City, Oklahoma, First, Second, and Third Awards

New Mexico Fiesta Biennial, Santa Fe, New Mexico, Honorable Mention

Philbrook Indian Art Exhibition, Philbrook Art Center, Tulsa, Oklahoma, First, Second, and Third Awards

Scottsdale National Indian Arts Exhibition, Scottsdale, Arizona, First, Second, and Third Awards

Tanner's All Indian Invitational Pottery and Painting Show, First Prize in Drawing

APPOINTMENTS

Board Member: Pacific Northwest Indian Center, Gonzaga University, Spokane, Washington

Board Member: Wheelwright Museum, Santa Fe, New Mexico

Fellow: Kellogg Fellowship Screening Committee, Navajo Health Authority, Window Rock, Arizona

Member: Four Corner States Art Conference

Standards Committee, Juror, New Mexico Arts and Crafts Fair

PHOTOGRAPHIC CREDITS
(in order of appearance)

Portrait of R. C. Gorman by Klaus Appel for *Mode Und Wohnen* magazine, Düsseldorf, Germany, 1978.

Gorman in his Navajo Gallery, Taos, 1970. Photograph by Joseph Farber.

Gorman at Tamarind Institute with printer Wayne Simpkins checking stone for *Starry Night*, 1971. Photograph, courtesy of Tamarind.

Gorman at Tamarind with printer Christopher Cordes checking proof of *Noon Meditation*, 1972. Photograph, courtesy of Tamarind.

Gorman with model Virginia Martinez in his Navajo Gallery-Studio, 1975. Photograph by J. B. Smith.

At Tamarind with printer Lynn Baker checking proof for *Rug No. 4* from *Homage to Spider Woman* suite, 1974. Photograph by Mel Buffington.

Gorman at Tamarind with printer Ben Q. Adams spraying liquid tusche on lithographic stone, 1975. Photograph by J. B. Smith.

At Editions Press with director Walter Maibaum and printer Richard Newlin checking drawn image on stone, 1976. Photograph by Ruffin A. Cooper, Jr.

Gorman taking a break at Western Graphics, 1977. Photograph by Kim Jew.

Comparing proofs with printer Richard Newlin at Editions Press, 1978. Photograph by Phillip Galgiani.

Index